ArtNotes Plus

Dixon Bennett
San Jacinto College

Janson's History of Art

The Western Tradition

Volume I

Seventh Edition

Penelope J. E. Davies
University of Texas at Austin

Walter B. Denny
University of Massachusetts at Amherst

Frima Fox Hofrichter
Pratt Institute

Joseph Jacobs
Independent Scholar and Art Critic

Ann M. Roberts
Lake Forest College

David L. Simon
Colby College

PEARSON

Prentice
Hall

Upper Saddle River, New Jersey 07458

© 2007 by PEARSON EDUCATION, INC.
Upper Saddle River, New Jersey 07458

10 9 8 7 6 5 4 3 2 1

ISBN 0-13-223961-2

Printed in the United States of America

Museum credits for fine art photos can be found with the images in the text. Please consult your textbook if you are studying the objects for identification purposes.

Contents

CHAPTER 1
Prehistoric Art

Janson, pp. 1–19

The earliest known images created by our direct ancestors date from about 40,000 years ago. They were hunter-gatherers who struggled to maintain adequate food, shelter, and population growth. These factors as well as a yearning to understand and control the world around them apparently led them to make often visually sophisticated magical and ritualistic images and objects.

NOTES

PALEOLITHIC ART

When does art first emerge?

Do experts agree about how and when the skill to create art was first established?

1.1. *Wounded Bison.* ca. 15,000–10,000 BCE. Altamira, Spain. (page 3)

What is unique about this and other works from Altimira?

1.2. *Lions and Bison*. End Chamber, Chauvet Cave. ca. 30,000–28,000 BCE. (page 3)

1.3. *Bear*. Recess of the Bears, Chauvet Cave. ca. 30,000–28,000 BCE. (page 3)

1.4. *Long-Eared Owl*. Chauvet Cave. ca. 30,000–28,000 BCE. (page 4)

Images of a variety of animals are found in cave art. How are the images painted, drawn, and incised on the walls of Chauvet Cave different from the images found in other caves such as Lascaux?

1.5. *Chinese Horse*. Lascaux Cave. ca. 15,000–13,000 BCE. (page 4)

How have the marks and shapes accompanying works such as this been interpreted?

How did the artists who created works such as this translate memory into natural appearance?

1.6. *Rhinoceros, Wounded Man, and Bison*. Lascaux Cave. ca. 15,000–13,000 BCE. (page 4)

What is so unique about this image containing a human form?

1.7. Schematic plan of Lascaux Cave system. (page 6)

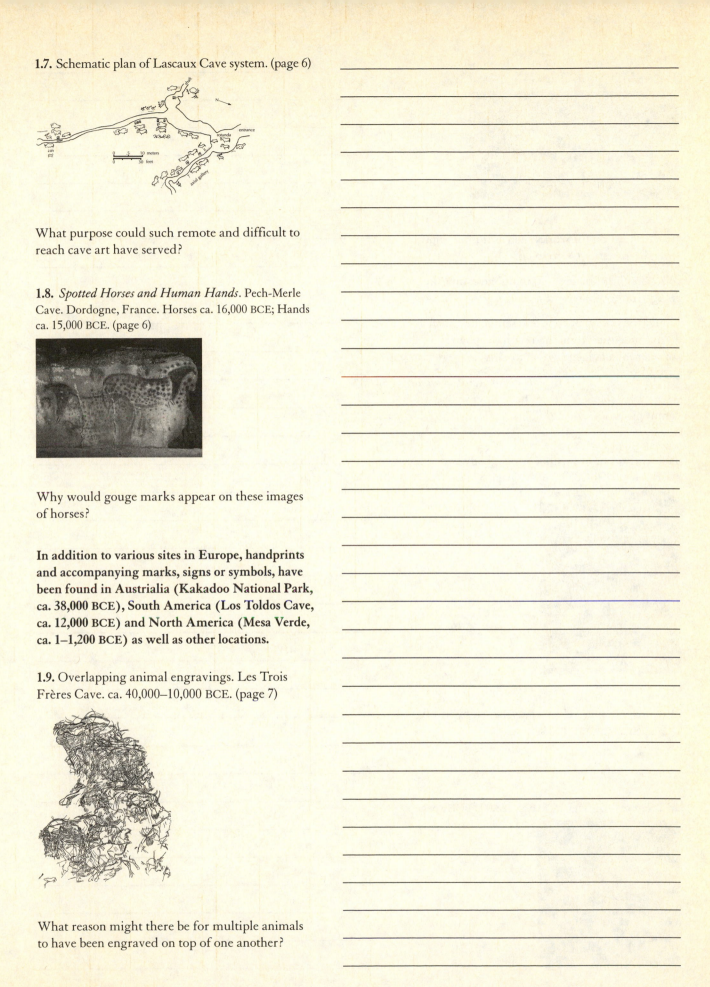

What purpose could such remote and difficult to reach cave art have served?

1.8. *Spotted Horses and Human Hands*. Pech-Merle Cave. Dordogne, France. Horses ca. 16,000 BCE; Hands ca. 15,000 BCE. (page 6)

Why would gouge marks appear on these images of horses?

In addition to various sites in Europe, handprints and accompanying marks, signs or symbols, have been found in Austrialia (Kakadoo National Park, ca. 38,000 BCE), South America (Los Toldos Cave, ca. 12,000 BCE) and North America (Mesa Verde, ca. 1–1,200 BCE) as well as other locations.

1.9. Overlapping animal engravings. Les Trois Frères Cave. ca. 40,000–10,000 BCE. (page 7)

What reason might there be for multiple animals to have been engraved on top of one another?

1.10. *Hall of the Bulls*. Lascaux Cave. ca. 15,000–10,000 BCE. (page 7)

The inspiration for works such as this has most often been attributed to what?

Why are these images said to utilize composite images rather than optical images?

Could the notion of chance resemblance, such as found in nature, combined with the powers of humans to imagine, have led to early image making?

Could works such as this and *Rhinoceros, Wounded Man, and Bison* (1.6.) from the same cave had different purposes?

1.11. Hybrid figure with a human body and feline head. ca. 40,000–28,000 BCE. (page 8)

What have some prehistorians named hybrid figures such as this one?

1.12. *Horse*. Vogelherd Cave. ca. 28,000 BCE. (page 9)

1.13. *Spear Thrower with Interlocking Ibexes*. Grotte d'Enlène. ca. 16,000 BCE. (page 9)

How were these three works created?

What links the *Vogelherd Horse* and the *Spear Thrower*?

1.14. *Two Bison*. Le Tuc d' Audoubert Cave. ca. 13,000 BCE. (page 9)

How might this work be compared to the *Chinese Horse* (1.5.) from Lascaux Cave?

1.15. *Dame à la Capuche (Woman from Brassempouy)*. Grotte du Pape. ca. 22,000 BCE. (page 11)

Does this work have anything in common with *Rhinoceros, Wounded Man, and Bison* (1.6.)?

1.16. *Woman of Willendorf.* ca. 28,000–25,000 BCE. (page 12)

How might these diminutive carvings of women be linked?

Note how similar representations of human figures continued to be created during the Neolithic period and later periods.

NEOLITHIC ART

Compare the Paleolithic period with the Neolithic period in terms of lifestyle and image making.

What new crafts and inventions were the results of Neolithic achievements?

1.17. Neolithic plastered skull. Jericho, Jordan. ca. 7000 BCE. (page 13)

Why are this object and like objects often described as "spirit traps"?

How may the Jericho skulls relate to earlier Paleolithic cave art?

1.18. Early Neolithic wall and tower. Jericho, Jordan. ca. 7000 BCE. (page 13)

What was first created because of this fortification system?

1.19. Human figures. Ain Ghazal, Jordan. ca. 6750–6250 BCE. (page 13)

What do these plaster figures constitute?

How might they be related to the Jericho plastered skulls?

1.20. Reconstruction of Çatal Hüyük, Turkey. (page 14)

Compare the architecture of Jericho and Çatal Hüyük. What do they have in common and how do they differ?

How do the burials at Çatal Hüyük relate to the burials at Jericho?

1.21. *Animal Hunt*. Restoration of Main Room, Shrine A.III.1. ca. 6000 BCE. Çatal Hüyük. (page 14)

How does this wall painting compare to Paleolithic works such as those found at Chauvet Cave and Lascaux Cave?

Why would both Paleolithic and Neolithic painted and drawn images of animals and humans primarily be depicted in profile?

1.22. *View of Town and Volcano*. ca. 6000 BCE. Wall painting. Shrine VII.14 Çatal Hüyük. (page 15)

What is so unique about this work?

1.23. Female and male figures. ca. 3500 BCE. Cernavoda, Romania. (page 16)

How do these works relate to the *Woman of Willendorf*? How are they different?

Could the differences between Paleolithic and Neolithic images stem from them having different purposes?

Define:
  megalith
  menhir
  dolmen
  post and lintel
  trilith
  chromlech

1.24. Menhir alignments at Ménec. ca. 4250–3750 BCE. Carnac, France. (page 17)

The lines' east-west orientation leads scholars to argue that they gauged what?

1.25. *Stonehenge* (aerial view). ca. 2100 BCE. Salisbury Plain, Wiltshire, England. (page 18)

Like Ménec, (1.24.) *Stonehenge* represents what?

The blocks are tailored to produce the same kind of refinements found in what other great architectural work?

1.26. Diagram of original arrangement of stones at *Stonehenge*. (page 18)

Many prehistorians believe that *Stonehenge* had two functions. What were they?

CHAPTER 2
Ancient Near Eastern Art

Janson, pp. 20 - 45

The end of the Neolithic Age and the beginnings of the Bronze Age saw the dawning of large scale communities for the first time. Between ca. 3500 BCE and ca. 200 BCE city-states developed in and around an area known as Mesopotamia in the Middle East. There was an almost constant ebb and flow of different city-states dominating the area beginning, for all intents and purposes, with Sumeria. Remarkably, Sumeria continued to influence virtually all that followed.

NOTES

SUMERIAN ART

2.1. Babylonian deed of sale. ca. 1750 BCE. (page 22)

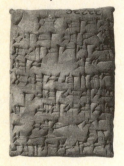

Define:
  pictogram
  cuneiform

Is our concept of history tied to the development of writing?

How did cuneiform writing help link the different groups that dominated the region at various times?

2.2. Remains of the "White Temple" on its ziggurat. ca. 3500–3000 BCE. Uruk (Warka), Iraq. (page 24)

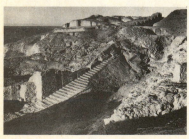

2.3. Plan of the "White Temple" on its ziggurat. (page 24)

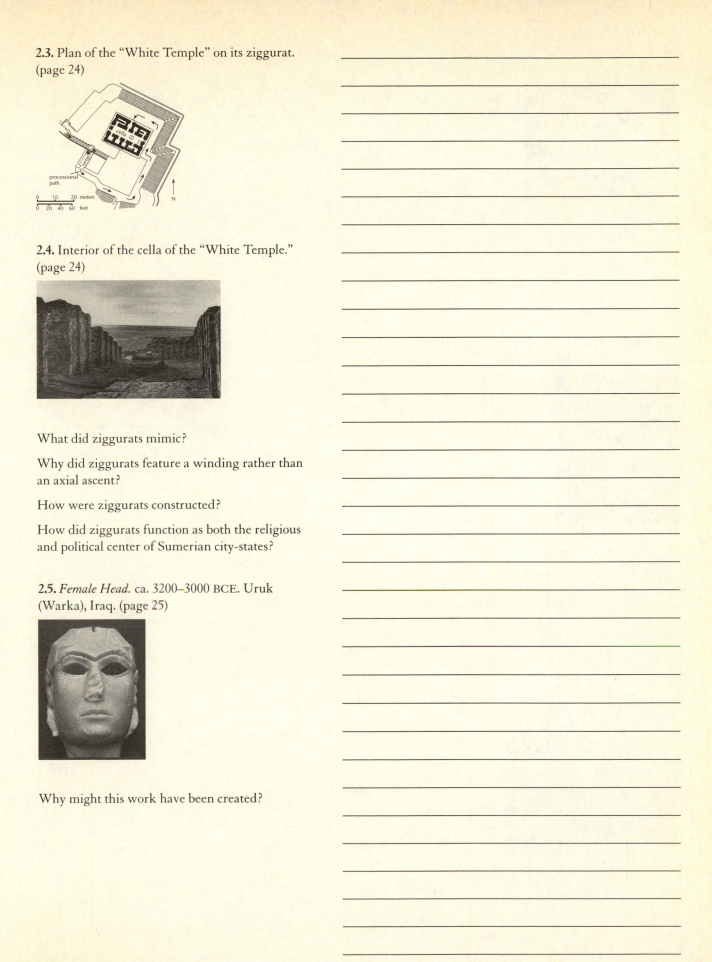

2.4. Interior of the cella of the "White Temple." (page 24)

What did ziggurats mimic?

Why did ziggurats feature a winding rather than an axial ascent?

How were ziggurats constructed?

How did ziggurats function as both the religious and political center of Sumerian city-states?

2.5. *Female Head.* ca. 3200–3000 BCE. Uruk (Warka), Iraq. (page 25)

Why might this work have been created?

2.6. Statues from the Abu Temple. ca. 2700–2500 BCE. Tell Asmar, Iraq. (page 26)

What do most scholars consider all figures such as these represent?

Why do these figures and the *Female Head* (2.5.) from Uruk probably have oversized eyes?

2.7. *Goat in Thicket* (*Ram and Tree*). ca. 2600 BCE. (page 26)

What was the probable reason that this work was created?

What does the combination of the goat and flowers apparently reflect?

2.8. *Royal Standard of Ur*, front and back sides. ca. 2600 BCE. (page 27)

Define:
  hieratic scale

How do the images on the *Royal Standard of Ur* contrast with Paleolithic cave paintings?

2.9. Bull Lyre, from the tomb of Queen Pu-abi. Ur (Muqaiyir), Iraq. ca. 2600 BCE. (page 28)

2.10. Inlay panel from the sound box of lyre, from Ur (Muqaiyir), Iraq. ca. 2600 BCE. (page 28)

Why might this inlay feature hybrid creatures and animals?

2.11. *Priest-King Feeding Sacred Sheep* from vicinity of Uruk (Warka), Iraq. ca. 3300 BCE. (page 29)

Cylinder seals provide important information about what?

ART OF AKKAD

2.12. *Head of an Akkadian Ruler* from Nineveh (Kuyunjik), Iraq. ca. 2250–2200 BCE. (page 29)

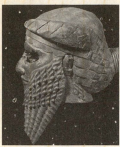

Discuss the medium employed. Why is the use of this medium so unusual?

How does this work show a link between the Akkadians and the Sumerians?

2.13. Stele of Naram-Sin. r. 2254–2218 BCE. (page 30)

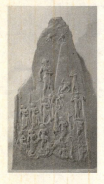

What does Naram-Sin's scale indicate?

How can the Stele of Naram-Sin be compared to the *View of Town* and *Volcano* (1.21.) from Çatal Hüyük?

NEO-SUMERIAN REVIVAL

2.14. Great ziggurat of King Urnammu. ca. 2100 BCE. Muqaiyir, Iraq. (page 31)

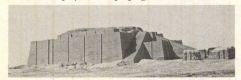

The concept of this ziggurat is obviously similar to the "White Temple" (2.2., 2.3., 2.4.) but how has it evolved?

2.15. Head of Gudea, from Lagash (Telloh), Iraq. ca. 2100 BCE. (page 32)

Why do we know that Gudea was enormously wealthy?

2.16. Seated statue of Gudea holding temple plan, from Girsu (Telloh), Iraq. ca. 2100 BCE. (page 32)

What do the rounded forms emphasize?

BABYLONIAN ART

2.17. Upper part of Stele inscribed with the Law Code of Hammurabi. ca. 1760 BCE. (page 33)

How does this work help legitimize Hammurabi's Law Code?

Does the style of the relief remind you of any earlier civilization?

2.18. Reconstruction drawing of the citadel of Sargon II, Dur Sharrukin (Khorsabad), Iraq. ca. 721–705 BCE. (page 35)

How did this complex express Assyrian royal power?

2.19. Gate of the Citadel of Sargon II, Dur Sharrukin. 742–706 BCE. (Khorsabad), Iraq. (page 35)

What do the lamassu represent?

What did the artists do to create the impression of total strength and stability from any direction?

2.20. *Fugitives Crossing River*, from the Northwest Palace of Ashurnasirpal II, Nimrud (Calah), Iraq. ca. 883–859 BCE. (page 36)

Define:
  Orthostats

2.21. Lion Hunt relief, from reign of Ashurbanipal ca. 645 BCE. (page 36)

Do the reliefs such as 2.20. and 2.21. reinforce the idea of Assyrian royal power and authority?

LATE BABYLONIAN ART

2.22. Ishtar Gate (restored), from Babylon, Iraq. ca. 575 BCE. (page 37)

What innovation did the Late Babylonians use to decorate the wall surfaces of their royal palaces?

REGIONAL NEAR EASTERN ART

2.23. The Lion Gate. Bogazköy, Anatolia (Turkey). ca. 1400 bce. (page 38)

What kind of tradition began with this gate?

What did these massive lions inspire?

2.24. Ivory plaque depicting a winged sphinx. Phoenician. ca. eighth century BCE. Found at Fort Shalmaneser, Nimrud (ancient Kalhu), northern Iraq. (page 39)

The Phoenicians incorporated ideas and motifs from what other cultures when creating their highly skilled metal and ivory work?

IRANIAN ART

2.25. Painted beaker, from Susa. ca. 5000–4000 BCE. (page 39)

What does the decoration on this painted ceramic beaker foretell?

2.26. Plan of Palace of Darius and Xerxes, Persepolis. 518–460 BCE. (page 40)

How does the design and construction of this palace result in a message of internationalism?

2.27. Rhyton. Achaemenid. 5th–3rd centuries BCE. (page 40)

Why does this rhyton also create an impression of internationalism?

2.28. Audience Hall of Darius and Xerxes, Persepolis, Iran. ca. 500 BCE. (page 41)

What various influences can be found in the ruins of this audience hall?

2.29. Bull capital, from Persepolis. ca. 500 BCE. (page 41)

Compare this column capital to Assyrian sculpture (especially 2.19.) as well as Persian crafts such as the Rhyton (2.27.).

2.30. *Darius and Xerxes Giving Audience*. ca. 490 BCE. (page 42)

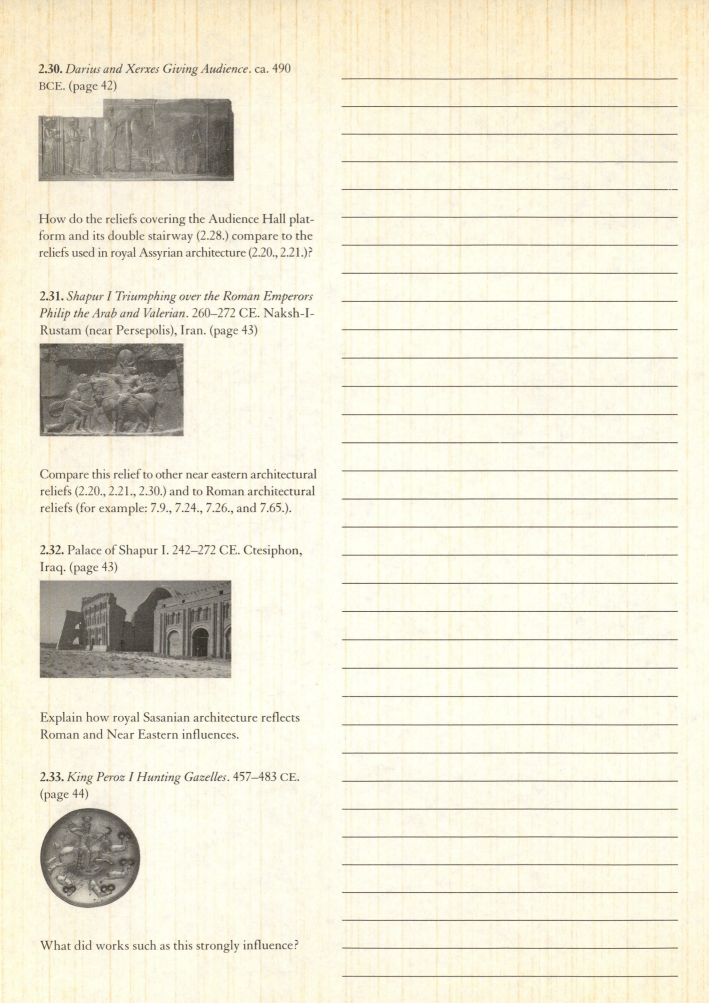

How do the reliefs covering the Audience Hall platform and its double stairway (2.28.) compare to the reliefs used in royal Assyrian architecture (2.20., 2.21.)?

2.31. *Shapur I Triumphing over the Roman Emperors Philip the Arab and Valerian*. 260–272 CE. Naksh-I-Rustam (near Persepolis), Iran. (page 43)

Compare this relief to other near eastern architectural reliefs (2.20., 2.21., 2.30.) and to Roman architectural reliefs (for example: 7.9., 7.24., 7.26., and 7.65.).

2.32. Palace of Shapur I. 242–272 CE. Ctesiphon, Iraq. (page 43)

Explain how royal Sasanian architecture reflects Roman and Near Eastern influences.

2.33. *King Peroz I Hunting Gazelles*. 457–483 CE. (page 44)

What did works such as this strongly influence?

CHAPTER 3
Egyptian Art

Janson, pp. 46–77

The Nile is one of the great rivers of the world. Like the Tigris and Euphrates in Mesopotamia, the Indus and Ganges in Pakistan and India, and the Huang Ho and Yangtze in China, the Nile helped give rise to one of the greatest civilizations the world has ever known. The ancient Egyptian civilization existed as a remarkably stable entity from ca. 3200 BCE until Alexander the Great conquered Egypt and founded Alexandria before he died in 323 BCE. The Egyptians' extreme reliance on religion and their belief in an afterlife was probably very instrumental in the remarkably constant art forms they created.

NOTES

PREDYNASTIC AND EARLY DYNASTIC ART

3.1. *Palette of King Narmer* from Hierakonpolis. ca. 3150–3125 BCE. (page 49)

Compare King Narmer to the leader or king on the *Royal Standard of Ur* (2.8.) and the stele of Naram-Sin (2.13.).

Define:
   hieroglyphs
   register
   ma'at

THE OLD KINGDOM: A GOLDEN AGE

3.2. Group of mastabas. (page 50)

mastaba

shafts

burial chamber

3.3. Imhotep. Step Pyramid and Funerary Complex of King Djoser, Saqqara. 3rd Dynasty. ca. 2681–2662 BCE. (page 50)

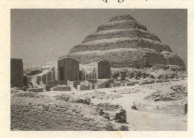

What is so important about Imhotep?

Compare Egyptian step pyramids to Mesopotamian ziggurats in terms of structure and use.

3.4. Plan of the funerary district of King Djoser, Saqqara. (page 51)

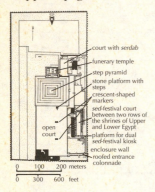

Why was this district located on the west side of the Nile?

What does the burial complex reproduce?

Define:
 ka
 sarcophagus

3.5. Transverse section of the Step Pyramid of King Djoser, Saggara. (page 51)

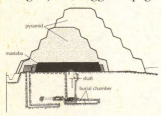

How might the progressively diminishing layers of masonry been used?

Define:
 serdab

3.6. Papyrus-shaped half-columns, North Palace, Funerary Complex of King Djoser, Saggara. (page 52)

What did the engaged columns in this view imitate?

3.7. The Pyramids of Menkaure ca. 2533–2515 BCE, Khafra ca. 2570–2544 BCE, and Khufu ca. 2601–2528 BCE. Giza. (page 53)

Define:
ben-ben

How was the orientation of the pyramids of Giza different from the funerary district of Saggara (3.3., 3.4.)?

Does this show a change in the way Egyptians conceived of their ruler?

3.8. North-south section of Pyramid of Khufu. (page 54)

silhouette of original facing stone
relieving blocks
airshaft?
airshaft?
grand gallery
king's chamber
thieves' tunnels
entrance
so-called queen's chamber
false tomb chamber

3.9. Model of the Great Pyramids at Giza: (1) Menkaure, (2) Khafra, (3) Khufu. (page 54)

3.10. The Great Sphinx. ca. 2570–2544 BCE. Giza. (page 55)

Scholars believe The Great Sphinx is a portrait of what king?

3.11. *Sculpture of Khafra*, from Giza. ca. 2500 BCE. (page 55)

How does this sculpture of Khafra set the standard for virtually all royal Egyptian free standing sculpture?

How does Egyptian royal sculpture compare to Mesopotamian royal sculpture?

3.12. *Sculpture of Menkaure and His Wife, Queen Khamerernebty II*, from Giza. ca. 2515 BCE. (page 56)

How well does this sculpture of Menkaure and his wife conform to the model created by the sculpture of Khafra (3.11.)?

3.13. *Sculpture of Prince Rahotep and His Wife, Nofret.* ca. 2580 BCE. (page 57)

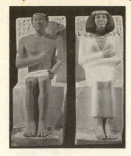

How did the sculptor of this work apparently compensate for this work having been carved from soft stone?

3.14. *Relief Panel of Hesy-ra*, from Saqqara. ca. 2600 BCE. (page 57)

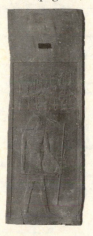

Compare Hesy-ra to King Narmer (3.1.)? What is consistent about their representations?

Define:
  Canon

3.15. *Sculpture of Seated Scribe*, from Saqqara. ca. 2400 BCE. (page 58)

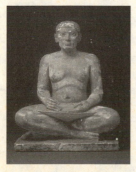

3.16. *Sculpture of Ka-Aper*, from Saqqara. ca. 2450–2350 BCE. (page 58)

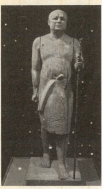

What is apparent about the sculpture of the Seated Scribe (3.15.) and the sculpture of Ka-Aper?

3.17. *Ti Watching a Hippopotamus Hunt*. ca. 2510–2460 BCE. (page 59)

What does this relief tell us about the representation of lower class Egyptian citizens or captives?

THE MIDDLE KINGDOM: REASSERTING TRADITION THROUGH THE ARTS

3.18. *Sculpture of Senwosret III* (fragment). ca. 1850 BCE. (page 59)

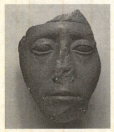

How does this depiction of Senwosret III show changes in Egyptian society during the Middle Kingdom?

3.19. *Sculpture of the Lady Sennuwy.* ca. 1920 BCE. (page 60)

Does this work indicate a change in the canon of proportion?

3.20. Rock-Cut Tombs at Beni Hasan, B-H 3–5, 11th and 12th Dynasties. ca. 1950–1900 BCE. (page 60)

3.21. Interior Hall of Rock-Cut Tomb, B-H 2, Beni Hasan. 12th Dynasty. ca. 1950-1900 BCE. (page 61)

How was this tomb (3.20. and 3.21.) designed and constructed?

3.22. *Feeding the Oryxes.* ca. 1928–1895 BCE. Detail of a wall painting. Tomb of Khnum-hotep, Beni Hasan. (page 61)

Describe how the workers feeding the oryxes are depicted?

3.23. Female Figurine, from Thebes. 12th–13th Dynasties. (page 62)

What might this figurine's functions have been?

Define:
   faience

THE NEW KINGDOM: RESTORED GLORY

3.24. Temple of Hatshepsut, Deir el-Bahri. ca. 1478–1458 BCE. (page 63)

How does this great temple link the temple with its environment?

3.25. Reconstruction of Temples, Deir el-Bahri, with temples of Mentuhotep II, Thutmose III, and Hatshepsut. (page 63)

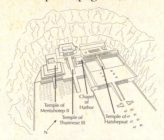

3.26. *Kneeling Figure of Queen Hatshepsut*, from Deir el-Bahri. ca. 1473–1458 BCE. (page 64)

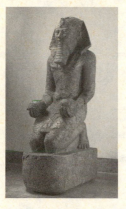

How did this sculpture, among others, attempt to help legitimize Queen Hatshepsut's rule?

3.27. Plan of Temple of Amun-Ra, Karnak, Thebes. (page 65)

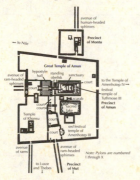

What was the metaphorical value of an Egyptian temple?

3.28. Hypostyle Hall of Temple of Amun-Ra. Karnak, Thebes. ca. 1290–1224 BCE. (page 65)

What do these great columns emulate?

Why did the architects make the columns even heavier than they needed to be?

3.29. *Seti I's Campaigns*, Temple of Amun at Karnak, Thebes (exterior wall, north side of hypostyle).ca. 1280 BCE. (page 66)

Define:
   sunken relief

3.30. Temple of Ramses, II, Abu Simbel. 19th Dynasty. ca. 1279–1213 BCE. (page 66)

What was so important about the original location of this temple and the location of a second complementary temple in honor of his wife?

3.31. Interior of Temple of Ramses II, Abu Simbel. 19th Dynasty. ca. 1279–1213 BCE. (page 67)

What is unusual about the columns on the interior of the temple?

3.32. *Sculpture of Senenmut with Nefrua*, from Thebes. ca. 1470–1460 BCE. (page 68)

What did this block statue function as?

3.33. *Musicians and Dancers*, fragment of a wall painting from the Tomb of Nebamun, Thebes. 1350 BCE. (page 69)

What is so unusual about the flute player and a clapper along with the nude dancers?

What may have influenced these changes?

3.34. *Mai and His Wife, Urel.* ca. 1375 BCE. Tomb of Ramose, Thebes. (page 69).

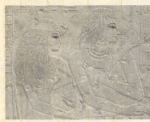

What is especially masterful about this wall relief?

How does it relate to the Old and Middle Kingdom depictions of similar subjects?

AKHENATEN AND THE AMARNA STYLE

3.35. *Sculpture of Akhenaten,* from Karnak, Thebes. 1353–1335 BCE. (page 70)

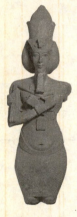

How does this work break with long-standing tradition?

Why was this new appearance probably created?

3.36. *Akhenaten and His Family.* ca. 1355 BCE. (page 71)

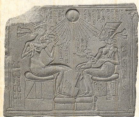

What is so remarkable about this relief?

3.37. *Sculpture of Queen Tiy*, from Kom Medinet el-Ghurab. ca. 1372 BCE. (page 71)

What delicate balance does the portrait of Akhenaten's mother strike?

3.38. *Sculpture of Queen Nefertiti*. ca. 1348–1336/5 BCE. (page 72)

What does this works' extraordinary elegance derive from?

3.39. Cover of the coffin of Tutankamen. 18th Dynasty. (page 73)

Why is Tutankamen so well remembered?

PAPYRUS SCROLLS:
THE BOOK OF THE DEAD

3.40. *The Weighing of the Heart and Judgement by Osiris*, from *The Book of the Dead of Hunefer*. 1285 BCE. (page 74)

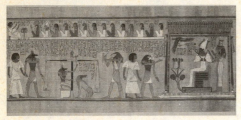

What did the *Books of the Dead* derive from?

What do they say about Egyptian's feelings about the traditions of their past?

LATE EGYPT

CHAPTER 4

Aegean Art

Janson, pp. 78–99

The Mediterranean and the Aegean seas have always been intimately bound as the major pathways for all of the people who have lived on or around these vital bodies of water. Three of the most interesting and enigmatic cultures the world has ever known were nourished during the third and second millennia BCE by their proximity to the Aegean. Most of what we have known about these cultures comes from ancient Greek writings and mythology. It is only in recent years that we have begun to truly acquire direct knowledge of these fascinating civilizations. They were greatly influenced by the cultures of the ancient Middle East and Egypt and they in turn influenced the civilizations that followed them, especially the Greeks and Romans.

NOTES

EARLY CYCLADIC ART

4.1. "Frying pan," from Chalandriani, Syros. Early Cycladic II. ca. 2500–220 BCE. (page 80)

How were works like this originally produced?

4.2. Figure, Cyclades. ca. 2500 BCE. (page 81)

What do figures such as this seem to look back to?

What did carved marble works such as this one appear to influence?

4.3. *Harpist*, from Amorgos, Cyclades. Latter part of the 3rd millennium BCE. (page 82)

How do works such as this one still look to other civilizations and the past for inspiration?

What is different about the depiction of this harpist?

MINOAN ART

4.4. Plan of the Palace Complex, Knossos, Crete. (Page 83)

What factors make this vast complex different from similar complexes in the Middle East [Citadel of Sargon II (2.18.) and the Palace of Darius and Xerxes (2.26.), for example] and in Egypt [Temple of Amun-Ra (3.27.)]?

4.5. Reconstruction of the Palace Complex, Knossos, Crete. (page 83)

What led later Greek legend to link this complex with the Labyrinth and the Minotaur?

4.6. Staircase, east wing, Palace Complex. ca. 1500 BCE. Knossos, Crete. (page 84)

What is so unique about the form of the columns in this view of the palace complex?

4.7. *Grandstand Fresco*, from Knossos, Crete. ca. 1500 BCE. (page 86)

Works such as this support the hypothesis that a great deal of what type of activity took place at the Palace Complex (4.4. and 4.5.)?

4.8. The Queen's Megaron. ca. 1700–1300 BCE. From Knossos, Crete. (page 87)

4.9. Spring Fresco. Akrotiri, Thera. ca. 1600–1500 BCE. (page 87)

How do the fresco in the Queen's Megaron (4.8.) and this fresco contrast with Egyptian murals and reliefs (3.17., 3.21., 3.22., 3.29. and 3.34.)?

4.10. *Flotilla* Fresco, from Akrotiri, Thera. ca. 1600–1500 BCE. (page 88)

What does this scene reflect?

4.11. Beaked jug (Kamares ware) from Phaistos. ca. 1800 BCE. (page 88)

What is revolutionary about Minoan pottery during the Middle and Late Periods?

What approach was taken when this jug was created?

4.12. *Octopus Vase*, stirrup jar from Palaikastro, Crete. ca. 1500 BCE. (page 89)

This work is a reflection of what kind of motifs prevalent during the Minoan Late Period?

4.13. *Harvestor Vase*, from Hagia Triada. ca. 1500–1450 BCE. (page 89)

What is so unique about this scene, whatever actual event is depicted?

Define:
   rhyton (rhyta)

4.14. Rhyton in the shape of a bull's head, from Khossos. ca. 1500–1450 BCE. (page 90)

What does the prevalence of the bull motif seem to suggest?

How have many of these vessels been found?

4.15. *Snake Goddess*, from the palace complex, Knossos. ca. 1650 BCE. (page 91)

Where was religious life on Minoan Crete apparently centered?

What may have been this statuettes' function?

4.16. *The Toreador Fresco*, from the palace complex, Knossos. ca. 1550–1450 BCE. (page 92)

Compare Minoan use of the convention of skin color in this work to the Egyptian sculpture of *Prince Rahotep and his Wife, Nofret* (3.13.).

Many scholars see the presence of women in prominent roles as evidence of what?

MYCENAEAN ART

4.17. Aerial view of Mycenae, Greece. ca.
1600–1200 BCE. (page 93)

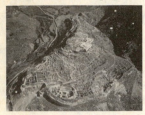

4.18. Aerial view of Tiryns, Greece. ca. 1400–1200
BCE. (page 93)

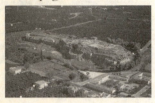

4.19. Plan of palace and citadel at Tiryns, Greece.
ca. 1400–1200 BCE. (page 93)

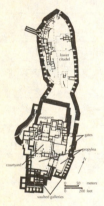

Compare the plans and views of Mycenae and
Tiryns to existing Minoan structures.

Define:
  megaron

4.20. Corbeled casemate at Tiryns, Greece. ca.
1400–1200 BCE. (page 95)

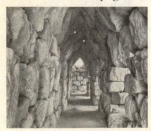

Define:
    corbel
    clopean

4.21. Drawing. Corbel Arch. (page 95)

Define:
    corbel arch

4.22. The Lion Gate, Mycenae, Greece. ca. 1250 BCE. (page 95)

What influences are evident in the relief and surrounding structure of The Lion Gate?

Define:
    heraldic pose

Why is this relief especially unique on the Greek mainland?

4.23. Reconstruction of megaron at Pylos. ca. 1300–1200 BCE. (page 96)

Reference page 110 in Chapter Five: Greek Art for a possible link between Mycenaen and Greek architecture.

4.24. "Treasury of Atreus," Mycenae, Greece. ca. 1300–1250 BCE. (page 96)

Define:
  dromos
  tholos
  corbel dome

4.25. Reconstruction of the façade of "Treasury of Atreus," Mycenae, Greece. ca. 1300–1250 BCE. (page 96)

What civilizations' architectural construction influenced the façade of the "Treasury of Atreus"?

4.26. Interior of "Treasury of Atreus," Mycenae, Greece. ca. 1300–1250 BCE. (page 97)

The "Treasury of Atreus" was the largest unsupported span in human history until what structure was built?

4.27. "Mask of Agamemnon," from a shaft grave in Circle A, Mycenae. ca. 1600–1500 BCE. (page 97)

4.28. Inlaid dagger blade, from shaft grave IV, Grave Circle A, Mycenae, Greece. ca. 1600–1550 BCE. (page 98)

What would the lions and their predatory strength be associated with?

4.29. *Vaphio Cups.* ca. 1500–1450 BCE. (page 98)

Artists from what civilization created or at least strongly influenced the creation of these cups?

4.30. "Three Deities," from Mycenae. 14th–13th century BCE. (page 99)

What are the very unique elements present in this tiny sculpture?

CHAPTER 5

Greek Art

Janson, pp. 100 – 159

The modern Western world owes a great debt to the ancient Greek civilization. Echoes of Greek cultural heritage swirl around us every day. It influences our art, as well as our politics, philosophy, and architecture.

Greek artists were constantly searching for better ways to express their belief in the aesthetic ideal. While they learned lessons from other cultures and the past, they were not content with simply following the ideas of others.

The danger inhabitants of the modern world face when approaching the ancient Greek world is to believe that because of the apparent familiarity of Greek works they must have retained the same meaning over the years.

THE EMERGENCE OF GREEK ART: THE GEOMETRIC STYLE

NOTES

5.1. Some common Greek vessel forms (page 103)

amphora   pelike   volute krater   krater   hydria   lekythos

amphora   kylix   skyphos   kantharos   aryballos

How are works in painted pottery and small-scale sculpture in clay and bronze related?

When did Greek potters develop an extensive, but fairly standardized, repertoire of vessel shapes?

5.2. Late Geometric belly-handled amphora by the Dipylon Master, from the Dipylon Cemetery, Athens. ca. 750 BCE. (page 104)

What was the original use for large vases such as this one?

What do the geometric designs on geometric style patterns reflect?

5.3. Common Greek ornamental motifs (page 104)

guilloche   acanthus

palmette   meander

rosette   egg-and-dart

Define:
   meander (maze or Greek key pattern)

What does the wide distribution of Greek Geometric pottery mean?

5.4. *Man and Centaur*, perhaps from Olympia. ca. 750 BCE. (page 105)

What does the figure's obvious interaction mean thematically?

THE ORIENTALIZING STYLE: HORIZONS EXPAND

5.5. The Ajax Painter. Aryballos (perfume jar). Middle Protocorinthian IA. 690–675 BCE. (page 106)

What does the Orientalizing style mean?

How does it relate to the development of narrative vase painting?

5.6. Geometric tripod cauldron from Olympia. 8th century. (page 106)

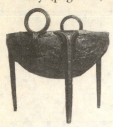

5.7. Griffin-head protome from a bronze tripod-cauldron, from Kameiros, Rhodes. ca. 650 BCE. (page 107)

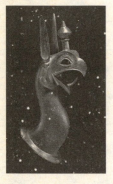

Define:
   protome

Why were bronze tripod cauldrons created?

ARCHAIC ART:
ART OF THE CITY-STATE

5.8. Ground plan of a typical Greek peripteral temple (page 109)

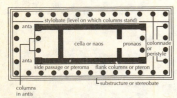

Define:
   peripteral temple
   peristyle
   Pronaos
   cella or noas
   in antis

5.9. Doric and Ionic styles in elevation (page 109)

What is the meaning of the term "architectural order"? Would the use of the term "type" be a better description of Greek architectural styles?

Why is understanding the definitions of the architectural elements used in the Doric and Ionic styles so important?

Compare the Doric and Ionic styles.

5.10. The Temple of Hera I ("Basilica"), ca. 550 BCE. and the Temple of Hera II ("Temple of Poseidon"), ca. 500 BCE. Paestum. (page 110)

What do some scholars think the Doric architectural elements guttae and mutule descend from?

How do these early Doric temples illustrate how much the style evolved in approximately 50 years?

5.11. Interior, Temple of Hera II. ca. 500 BCE. (page 111)

Define:
  entasis

5.12. Sectional view (restored) of the Temple of Aphaia, Aegina. (page 111)

Why would Greek architects have supported the ceiling of temples such as these with two rows of columns with each supporting a smaller set of columns (as seen in 5.11. and here)?

5.13. Restored plan of the Temple of Artemis at Ephesos, Turkey. ca. 560 BCE. (page 112)

How long after the Doric did the Ionic style appear?

What seems to have strongly inspired the Ionic style?

Define:
  dipteral

5.14. *Kore (Maiden)*. ca. 630 BCE. (page 113)

Define:
  kore
  korai

How does Greek archaic figurative sculpture show an Egyptian influence?

5.15. *Kouros (Youth)*. ca. 600–590 BCE. (page 113)

Define:
  kouros
  kouroi

How does this and similar Greek works move beyond Egyptian sculpture?

What makes the most sense when trying to explain why Greek Archaic figurative sculpture was created?

5.16. *Kroisos (Kouros from Anavysos)*. ca. 540–525 BCE. (page 114)

Define:
  Archaic smile

Why do most authorities think this work is a later work than the previous Kouros (5.15.)?

This and like works are the earliest stone human figurative images in the history of art to do what?

5.17. *Kore in Dorian Peplos,* known as *Peplos Kore*. ca. 530 BCE. (page 115)

49

5.18. *Kore*, from Chios (?). ca. 520 BCE. (page 115)

Explain how the *Kore in Dorian Peplos* (5.17.) and the *Kore* from Chios show the development of Greek figure types through the Archaic period?

What role does color play in sculptures of korai and kouroi?

5.19. Central portion of the west pediment of the Temple of Artemis at Corfu, Greece. ca. 600–580 BCE. (page 116)

To what does this work hold a debt?

How might this solution to the triangular shape be not wholly satisfactory?

5.20. Reconstruction drawing of the west front of the Temple of Artemis at Carfo (page 116)

5.21. Reconstruction drawing of the Treasury of the Siphnians. Sanctuary of Apollo at Delphi. ca. 525 BCE. (page 117)

Define:
  caryatid

5.22. *Battle of the Gods and Giants*, from the north frieze of the Treasury of the Siphnians, Delphi. ca. 520 BCE. (page 117)

5.23. Reconstruction drawing of the east pediment of the Temple of Aphaia, Aegina. (page 118)

Using the Temple of Artemis at Corfu (5.19., 5.20.), the Treasury of the Siphnians at Delphi (5.21., 5.22.) and the Temple of Aphaia at Aegina (5.23., 5.24., 5.25.) as models, discuss the development of architectural sculpture in Greek temple design.

5.24. Dying Warrior, from the west pediment of the Temple of Aphaia. ca. 500–490 BCE. Marble. (page 118)

5.25. Dying Warrior, from the east pediment of the Temple of Aphaia. ca. 480 BCE. (page 119)

How does this Dying Warrior vary from the previous Dying Warrior (5.25.) from the opposite end of the same temple?

5.26. *Achilles and Ajax Playing Dice*. Black-figured amphora signed by Exekias as painter and potter. ca. 540–530 BCE. (page 120)

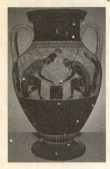

Why did Greek vase painters develop the black figure style? When did this development occur?

Describe the strengths and weaknesses of the black figure style.

5.27. Euthymides. *Dancing Revelers*. Red-figured amphora. ca. 510–500 BCE. (page 121)

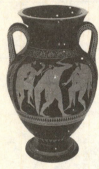

Describe the red figure style and explain why and when it replaced the black figure style.

5.28. Douris Painter. *Eos and Memnon*. Interior of an Attic red-figured kylix. ca. 490–480 BCE. (page 121)

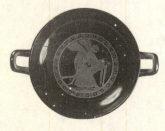

What is the core of this image?

THE CLASSICAL AGE

5.29. *Kritios Boy*. ca. 480 BCE. (page 122)

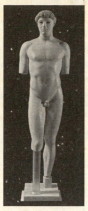

Define:
  contrapposto

The *Kritios Boy* marks a critical point in Greek art. Explain the radical innovations the sculptor of the *Kritios Boy* wrought.

5.30. Charioteer from Motya, Sicily. ca. 450–440 BCE. (page 122)

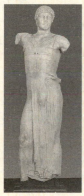

How did this sculptor use the fine fabric clothing the Charioteer?

5.31. *Zeus or Poseidon*. ca. 460–450 BCE. (page 123)

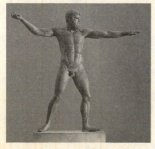

What did this sculptor capture in a single figure?

5.32. *Diskobolos (Discus Thrower)*. Roman marble copy after a bronze original of ca. 450 BCE. by Myron. (page 125)

If *Zeus or Poseidon* (5.31.) showed the strides made in the development of Greek Classical sculpture, what does Myron achieve with this work?

5.33. *Doryphoros (Spear Bearer)*. Roman copy after an original of ca. 450–440 BCE. by Polykleitos. (page 125)

With this work Polykleitos made what proposal?

This proposal was rooted in what philosophical quest?

5.34. Riace Warrior A, found in the sea off Riace, Italy. ca. 450 BCE. (page 126)

What is so unusual about this work?

5.35. Photographic reconstruction (partial) of the *Battle of the Lapiths and Centaurs*, from the west pediment of the Temple of Zeus at Olympia. ca. 460 BCE. Marble, slightly over life-size. (page 127)

What is different in this grouping from the pedimental figures from the Temple of Aphaia (5.23., 5.24., 5.25.).

What is the basis for the conflict apparent in this relief?

5.36. *Atlas Bringing Herakles the Apples of the Hesprides*. ca. 460 BCE. (page 128)

5.37. Akropolis (view from the west), Athens. The Propylaea, 437–432 BCE; with the Temple of Athena Nike, 427–424 BCE. (page 129)

What have the structures on the Akropolis come to exemplify?

Identification:
  Pericles
  Phidias

5.38. Plan of the Akropolis at Athens in 400 BCE. (page 129)

In creating these monuments artists continued to grapple with ways of creating harmony through what principles?

5.39. Iktinos and Kallikrates. The Parthenon (view from the west). Akropolis, Athen. 447–432 BCE. (page 130)

What makes the Parthenon such an extraordinarily sophisticated building?

Describe how a mathematical formula was used to create the harmonious proportions found in the Parthenon.

How did the architects deviate from that formula?

5.40. Model of *Athena Parthenes*, by Phidias. ca. 438 BCE. (page 131)

Define:
    chryselephantine

What makes the Parthenon something besides an ideal Doric temple?

5.41. Jacques Carrey. Drawings of the east pediment of the Parthenon. 1674 CE. (page 133)

Why is this drawing so important?

5.42. Dionysos from the east pediment of the Parthenon. ca. 438–432 BCE. (page 134)

What gives this figure so much implied power?

5.43. Three Goddesses, from the east pediment of the Parthenon. ca. 438–432 BCE. (pages 133)

What kind of effect does the fabric struggling with the three goddesses' legs create?

5.44. Lapith and Centaur, metope from the south side of the Parthenon. ca. 440 BCE. Marble. Height 56". (page 134)

5.45. *Lapith and Centaur*, metope from the south side of the Parthenon. ca. 440 BCE. Marble. (page 134)

What do the four metope cycles on the Parthenon depict?

5.46. Frieze above the western entrance of the cella of the Parthenon. ca. 440–432 BCE. (Page 135)

5.47. *Horsemen* from the west frieze of the Parthenon. ca. 440–432 BCE. (page 135)

What do frenzied animals such as these rearing horses effectively emphasize?

5.48. East frieze of the Parthenon. ca. 440 BCE. (page 135)

This part of the Parthenons' Ionic frieze is the most problematic when scholars attempt to interpret its meaning. What are the most prevalent theories?

5.49. *Nike*, from the balustrade of the Temple of Athena Nike. ca. 410–407 BCE. (page 137)

Whose sculptural style continues to have a great deal of influence over works such as this?

5.50. *Grave Stele of Hegeso*. ca. 410–400 BCE. (page 137)

What does the relief merging with the background strengthen?

This stele is a particulary good example of what?

5.51. Mnesikles. The Propylea, 437–432 BCE. (view from the west). Akropolis, Athens. (page 138)

How did Mnesikles adapt elements of a Doric temple to create the Propylea?

The Propylea contains a public room designed to do what for the first time?

5.52. Temple of Athena Nike. 421–405 BCE. (view from the east). Akropolis, Athens. (page 139)

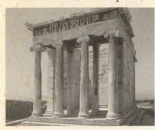

Why may Pericles have wanted elements of the Ionic style added to the Akropolis?

5.53. The Erechtheion. 421–405 BCE. (view from the southeast). Akropolis, Athens. (page 139)

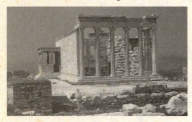

What was the major challenge for the architect of the Erechtheion?

THE LATE CLASSICAL PERIOD

5.54. Theater, Epidauros, Early third to second centuries BCE. (page 140)

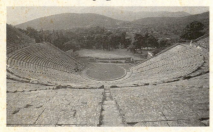

5.55. Plan of the Theater, Epidauros. (page 140)

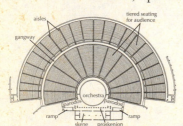

5.56. Reconstruction drawing of the Mausoleum at Halikarnassos. ca. 359–351 BCE. (page 141)

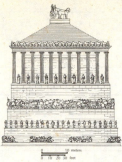

As one of the wonders of the ancient world, how can the Mausoleum at Halikarnassos be considered a preview of late Greek art and architecture and feelings about leaders or rulers?

5.57. Corinthian style in elevation. (page 142)

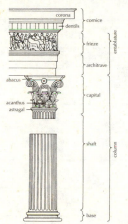

Where is the first place that Corinthian columns appeared?

5.58. Polykleitos the Younger. Corinthian capital, from the Tholos at Epidauros. ca. 350 BCE. (page 142)

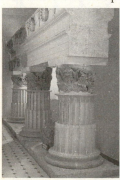

These particular Corinthian capital remains continue what tradition, begun with the Parthenon?

5.59. Head of Herakles or Telephos, from the west pediment of the Temple of Athena Alea, Tegea. ca. 340 BCE. (page 143)

What is new and important about this late Classical sculpture?

5.60. *Aphrodite of Knidos*. Roman copy of an original of ca. 340–330 BCE. by Praxiteles. (page 143)

How was the original of this work absolutely unique?

5.61. *Hermes*. Roman copy after an original of ca. 320–310 BCE. by Praxiteles. (page 144)

How was this work by Praxiteles different than the Doryphorus (5.33.) by Polykleitos?

5.62. *Apoxyomenos (scraper)*. Lysippos. Roman marble copy, probably after a bronze original of ca. 330 BCE. (page 144)

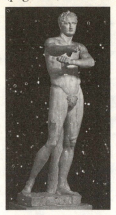

Compare the proportion of this work to the proportion of the *Doryphorus*.

What device did Lysippos use that was symptomatic of a new interest in illusionism?

5.63. Niobid Painter. Red-figured calyx krater, from Orvieto. ca. 460–450 BCE. (page 145)

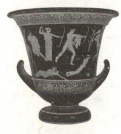

What did the Niobid Painter do that was new about the way he arranged the figures on this calyx?

5.64. Reed Painter. White-ground lekythos. ca. 425–400 BCE. (page 145)

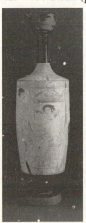

What did the freedom of technique allowed by white-ground vase painting allow the Reed Painter to explore?

THE AGE OF ALEXANDER AND THE HELLENISTIC PERIOD

5.65. Pytheos, plan of Temple of Athena, Priene. 334 CE. (page 146)

What did Vitruvius fault Pytheos for?

5.66. Paionios of Ephesos and Daphnis of Miletos. Temple of Apollo. Didyma, Turkey. Begun 313 BCE. (page 147)

5.67. Plan of Paionios of Ephesos and Daphnis of Miletos, Temple of Apollo, Didyma, Turkey. Begun 313 BCE. (page 147)

How is this temple an excellent example of the theatricality of Hellenistic Architecture?

5.68. Model of the city of Priene, 4th century BCE. and later. (page 148)

What is the most dominant factor in the design of the city of Priene?

5.69. Plan of Pergamon, Turkey (page 149)

How was the plan of the city of Pergamon different from the plan of the city of Priene?

5.70. Lysippos. *Portrait of Alexander the Great, the "Azara herm."* Roman copy after an original of the late 4th century BCE. (page 150)

Who was one of the major catalysts in the continued flourishing of portraiture as a major branch of Greek sculpture?

5.71. *Portrait Head* from Delos. ca. 80 BCE. (page 150)

What is so rare about this *Portrait Head*?

5.72. Epigonos of Pergamon (?) *Dying Trumpeter*. Perhaps a Roman copy after a bronze original of ca. 230–220 BCE.

How does the *Dying Trumpeter* communicate empathetically?

5.73. The west front of the Great Altar of Zeus at Pergamon (restored). (page 152)

What is especially unique about this massive altar?

5.74. *Athena and Alkyoneus,* from the east side of the Great Frieze of the Great Altar of Zeus at Pergamon. ca. 166–156 BCE. (page 152)

What is captured for the first time in this *Great Frieze*?

5.75. Pythokritos of Rhodes (?). *Nike of Samothrace*. ca. 190 BCE. (page 153)

What is so special about this work? How does it interact with its environment?

What term do scholars use to describe both the *Nike of Samothrace* and the *Great Altar of Zeus*?

5.76. *Aphrodite, Pan, and Eros*. ca. 100 BCE. (page

What was the sculptor of this work attempting to do?

5.77. *Drunken Old Woman*. Roman copy of an original of late 3rd or late 2nd century BCE. (page 155)

What genre of Hellenistic sculpture does this work represent?

5.78. *The Abduction of Persephone*. Detail of a wall painting in Tomb I, Vergina, Macedonia. ca. 340–330 BCE. (page 157)

What can we tell about Hellenistic wall painting from *The Abduction of Persephone*?

5.79. *The Battle of Issus or Battle of Alexander and the Persians.* ca. 100 BCE. Mosaic copy from Pompeii of a Hellenistic painting of ca. 315. BCE. (page 158)

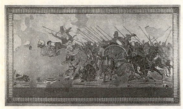

What techniques of Hellenistic wall painting are apparent in this masterful Pompeian floor mosaic?

CHAPTER 6
Etruscan Art

Janson, pp. 160–175

The Etruscans were flourishing on the Italian peninsula while the Greeks were in their Archaic period. Some think they originated in Asia Minor ca. 1200 BCE. Others feel they were indigenous to the Italian mainland. Whatever their origins, the Etruscans as sailors and merchants were able to create a culture rich with influences from the East and from Greece. They made major artistic contributions and were a strong influence, along with Greece, on the later Roman civilization.

NOTES

FUNERARY ART

6.1. Fibula from Regolini-Galassi Tomb. Cerveteri. ca. 670–650 BCE.

This work helps highlight the Etruscans' magnificent goldsmithing art. What probably influenced the motifs used?

6.2. Aerial view of part of Banditaccia Cemetery. 7th–2d centuries BCE.

How did the Etruscans create their "tumulus tombs"?

6.3. Plan of Tomb of the Shields and Chairs. ca. 550–500 BCE. (page 163)

6.4. Burial chamber, Tomb of the Reliefs. 3rd century BCE. (page 165)

What did scholars tend to believe that these burial chambers (6.3. and 6.4.) evoked?

Are they furnished in a way that reminds of another civilization?

6.5. Tomb of Hunting and Fishing. ca. 520 BCE. (page 166)

What do wall paintings such as 6.5. (Archaic Period) and 6.6. (Classical Period) reveal about the subject matter used in most Etruscan tombs?

6.6. Tomb of the Triclinium. ca. 470–460 BCE. (page 166)

How are Etruscan wall paintings different from Greek wall paintings, especially landscape scenes?

6.7. Tomb of Orcus. 350–300 BCE. (page 167)

Explain how this work illustrates some of the changes in Etruscan tomb paintings during their Late Classical period.

6.8. Human-headed cinerary urn. ca. 675–650 BCE. (page 167)

How does this cinerary urn represent the norm during the early or Orientalizing period of the Etruscan culture?

6.9. Sarcophagus, from Cerveteri. ca. 520 BCE. (page 168)

Define:
  terra cotta

How does the use of terra cotta influence the form of this sarcophagus?

6.10. *Youth and Female Demon*. Cinerary container. Early 4th century BCE. (page 168)

Why do we know that the woman sitting at the foot of the couch in this Etruscan cinerary container is not the young man's wife?

6.11. Funerary urns in the Inghirami tomb. Hellenistic period. (page 169)

Why did wealthy Etruscans apparently continue to bury their dead together in family tombs?

6.12. Sarcophagos lid of Larth Tetnies and Thanchvil Tarnai. ca. 350–300 BCE. (page 169)

What other culture is reflected in this Etruscan sarcophagus lid?

6.13. Porta Marzia. 2nd century BCE. (page 170)

Define:

voussoir

What is the arch in the Porta Marzia visual proof of?

6.14. Plan of residential complex. 6th century BCE. (page 170)

This kind of architecture was possibly the conceptual forerunner of what?

6.15. Reconstruction of an Etruscan temple, as described by Vitruvius. (page 170)

How did the design and materials of an Etruscan temple differ from an equivalent Greek temple?

6.16. *Apollo (Aplu)*, from Veii. ca. 510 BCE. (page 171)

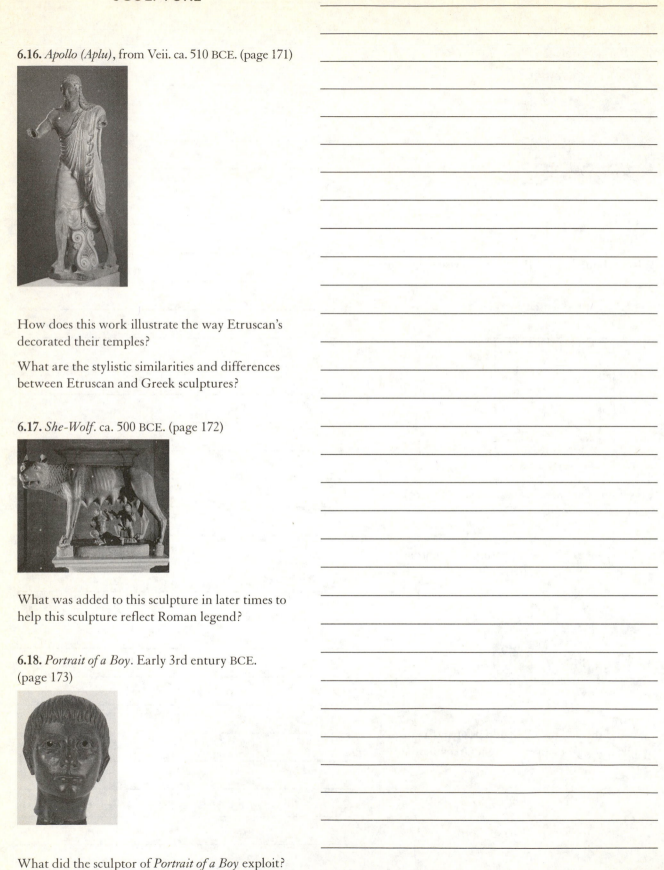

How does this work illustrate the way Etruscan's decorated their temples?

What are the stylistic similarities and differences between Etruscan and Greek sculptures?

6.17. *She-Wolf*. ca. 500 BCE. (page 172)

What was added to this sculpture in later times to help this sculpture reflect Roman legend?

6.18. *Portrait of a Boy*. Early 3rd entury BCE. (page 173)

What did the sculptor of *Portrait of a Boy* exploit?

6.19. *Aule Meteli (L'Arringatore).* Early 1st century BCE. (page 173)

Why is it rather apparent that this sculpture was created by an Etruscan artist?

What kind of questions are raised by this sculpture?

6.20. Engraved back of a mirror. ca. 400 BCE. (page 174)

What kind of scene is portrayed on the back of this bronze mirror?

Why were mirrors like this valued by the Etruscans?

CHAPTER 7
Roman Art

Janson, pp. 176–229

Roman art and architecture are more available to the modern world than any other civilization of the past. At the height of its power, the Roman Empire cloaked most of the Western world from Northern Europe to North Africa from the Near East to the British Isles. The Romans were able to expand so dramatically because they were tolerant of non-Roman cultures. They absorbed the best ideas, arts, and innovations of these cultures and melded them together to create great art, architecture, engineering, and urban planning that in many ways is still relevant today.

NOTES

EARLY ROME AND THE REPUBLIC

7.1. Restored plan of Temple of Jupiter Optimus Maximus. Dedicated ca. 509 BCE. (page 180)

What influences are seen in this great early temple plan and recent excavations?

7.2. Temple of Portunus, Rome. ca. 80–70 BCE. (page 180)

What sets this well preserved temple apart from Classical Greek temples?

7.3. Arch, barrel vault, and groin vault. (page 181)

What other cultures were aware of and used the arch and barrel vault?

How did the Romans use the arch, barrel vault, and groin vault?

7.4. Diagram illustrating Roman concrete facings. (page 181)

What is so important about the Roman development of concrete?

The history of Roman architecture is a dialogue between what two ways of building?

7.5. Porticus Aemilia, Rome. First half of the 2d century BCE. (page 182)

This building was the earliest known building in Rome to be constructed of what building material?

7.6. Sanctuary of Fortuna Primigenia, Praeneste. Early 1st century BCE. (page 182)

How did the Sanctuary integrate itself into the hillside it is now a part of?

7.7. Axonometric reconstruction of the Sanctuary of Fortuna. Primigenia, Praeneste. (page 183)

How did the architects of the Sanctuary of Fortuna employ concrete?

7.8. Theater Complex of Pompey, Rome. Dedicated in 55 BCE. (page 184)

How did Pompey, like Sulla and Julius Caesar after him, use architecture?

How was concrete used to construct this theater? In what way was this theater a first?

7.9. Sculptural reliefs from statue base, showing sea thiasos and census. So-called Altar of Domitius Ahenobarbus or Statue Base of Marcus Antonius. Late 2d to early 1st century BCE. (page 185)

How did the Romans use commerative sculpture (freestanding and relief) differently than the Greeks?

7.10. *Brutus*. Late 4th or early 3rd century BCE. (page 187)

How is this bronze portrait of Brutus different from even Hellenistic Greek portrait sculpture or the *Head of an Akkadian Ruler* (2.12.)?

7.11. Veristic male portrait. Early 1st century BCE. (page 188)

How does this work go even further than *Brutus* (7.10.) in creating an ideal Roman portrait sculpture?

7.12. *Pompey*. ca. 50 BCE. (page 189)

What earlier ruler is alluded to with this portrait of *Pompey*?

7.13. Togate male portrait with busts. Late 1st century BCE. (page 189)

What Roman practice may have inspired this sculpture?

7.14. Funerary relief of the Gessii. ca. 50 BCE. (page 190)

What kind of individuals are portrayed in this relief?

7.15. Esquiline tomb painting. Late 4th or early 3rd century BCE. (page 190)

What did Roman generals make a practice of commissioning?

7.16. *Augustus of Primaporta*. Possibly Roman copy of a statue of ca. 20 CE. (page 191)

This portrait combines a series of references to what? What Classical Greek sculpture probably directly influenced this portrait?

THE EARLY EMPIRE

7.17. *Portrait of Livia*, from the Fayum. After 14 CE. (page 192)

This portrait of *Livia* resembles images of what?

7.18. *Portrait of Vespasian*. ca. 75 CE. (page 192)

This *Portrait of Vespasian* shows a return to what?

7.19. *Portrait of Hadrian*. After 117 CE. (page 193)

This *Portrait of Hadrian*, in contrast to the *Portrait of Vespasian* (7.18.), moves in the direction of what style?

7.20. *Portrait of Domitia Longina*. Late 1st century CE. (page 193)

Domitia Longina's hairstyle and the way it was carved and drilled reflected what?

7.21. *Equestrian statue of Marcus Aurelius*. 161–180 CE. (page 194)

This spectacular equestrian portrait shows how Roman portraits took on what kind of quality beginning in the second half of the second century CE? Who did Christians mistakenly think this work portrayed?

7.22. *Portrait of Faustina the Younger*. ca. 147–148 CE. (page 195)

Does the portrait of the wife of Marcus Aureliius remind of the *Portrait of Livia*? Is it different in any way?

7.23. Ara Pacis Augustae, west facade. 13–9 BCE. (page 195)

7.24. Ara Pacis Augustae, Imperial Procession south frieze. 13–9 BCE. (page 196)

Together the reliefs from the Ara Pacis Augustae embody what? They bear a superficial resemblance to what earlier reliefs?

7.25. Arch of Titus. ca. 81 CE. (page 196)

7.26. Relief in bay of Arch of Titus. ca. 81 CE. (page 197)

Why were arches like the Arch of Titus erected? Where were they often placed?

7.27. Relief in bay of Arch of Titus. ca. 81 CE. (page 198)

What do the reliefs on the Arch of Titus express?

7.28. Column of Trajan, Rome. 106–113 CE. (page 199)

Define:
belvedere

How does the relief on the Column of Trajan surpass the visual narratives of military conquests of the Assyrians (2.20.) and the Egyptians (3.29.)?

7.29. Lower portion of the Column of Trajan.
106–113 CE. (page 199)

What became full-blown in the Column of Trajan?

7.30. Column base of Antoninus Pius and Faustina.
Apotheosis relief. ca. 161 CE. (page 200)

7.31. Column base of Antoninus Pius and Faustina.
Decursio relief. ca. 161 CE. (page 201)

What begins to happen visually in this column base
(7.30. and 7.31.)?

7.32. Funerary relief of a butcher and a woman.
Mid-2d century CE. (page 201)

How is the treatment of this relief different from
the panels of the Arch of Tius (7.25., 7.26., 7.27.)?

85

7.33. Plan of the Imperial Forums, Rome. (page 202)

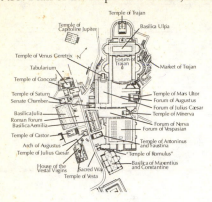

Why were all of these forums located so close together?

7.34. Forum of Augustus, Rome. Dedicated in 2 BCE. (page 202)

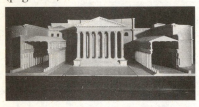

How did Augustus use the forum named after him to enhance his position?

7.35. Forum of Trajan, Rome. (page 203)

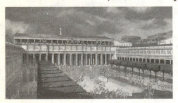

How does the Forum of Trajan stand apart from the other forums grouped around it? It adapted the features from which other forum?

7.36. Colosseum, Rome. 72–80 CE. (page 204)

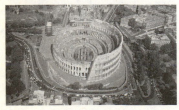

Who constructed the Colosseum? What was new about this structure?

7.37. Colosseum, sectional view. (page 204)

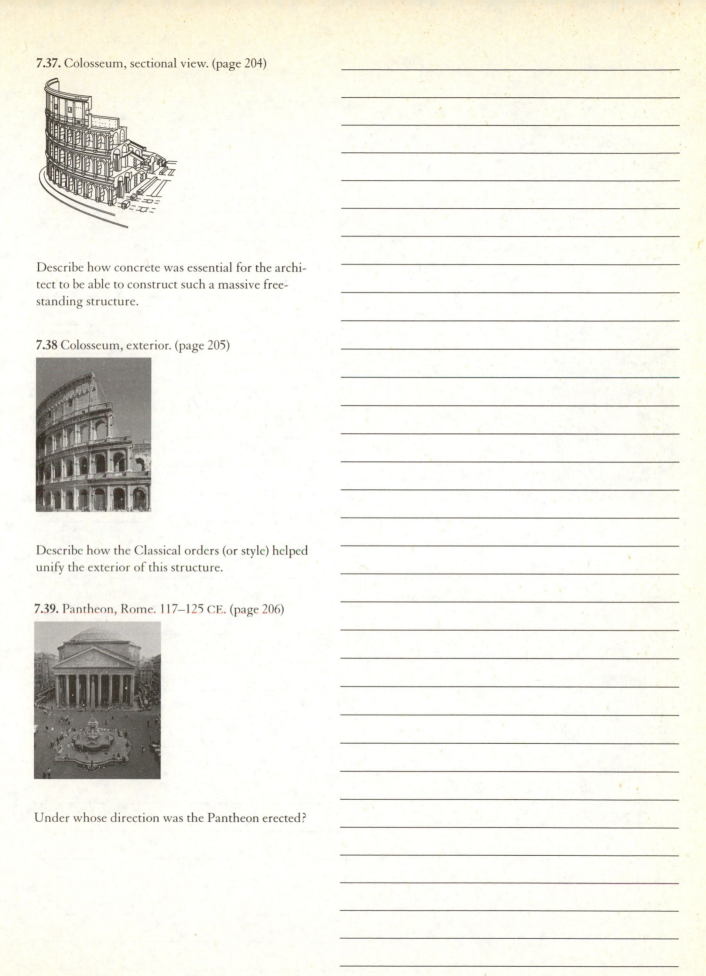

Describe how concrete was essential for the architect to be able to construct such a massive freestanding structure.

7.38 Colosseum, exterior. (page 205)

Describe how the Classical orders (or style) helped unify the exterior of this structure.

7.39. Pantheon, Rome. 117–125 CE. (page 206)

Under whose direction was the Pantheon erected?

7.40. Pantheon, Rome. Schematic drawing (page 206)

During Roman times how would a visitor have approached the Pantheon?

7.41. Pantheon, Rome, Interior. (page 207)

Define:
  oculus
  coffer

How did the architect calibrate the kind of concrete used to create the dome?

7.42. Plan of the Pantheon (page 207)

Define:
  drum

What variants in the design of the Pantheon give the structure its unique appeal?

7.43. Transverse section of the Pantheon. (page 208)

How do the dome and the drum of the Pantheon relate to one another?

7.44. Scenic Canal, Hadrian's Villa at Tivoli, ca. 130–138 CE. (page 208)

What did the designer or architect of Hadrian's Villa at Tivoli do to make the Villas' forms appear to follow the natural line of the landscape?

7.45. Aqueduct, Segovia, 1st or early 2d century CE. (page 209)

What effect did Roman aqueducts have on the landscape they crossed?

ART AND ARCHITECTURE
IN THE PROVINCES

7.46. Maison Carrée, Nîmes. Early 2d century CE(?). (page 210)

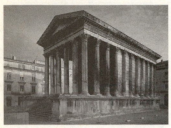

Compare Maison Carrée to the Temple of Portunus, Rome. (7.2.).

7.47. El Khasneh, Petra, Jordon. Probably early 2d century CE. (page 211)

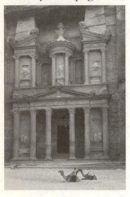

Define:
  living rock

Roman styles combined with what kind of building tradition to create this powerfully effective facade?

7.48. Funerary relief of Tibnan, from Palmyra, Syria. ca. 150–200 CE. (page 211)

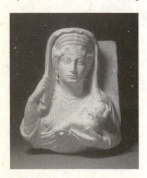

What does this funerary portrait neatly encapsulate?

7.49. Portrait of a Woman, from Hawara in the Fayum, Lower Egypt. ca. 110–130 CE. (page 213)

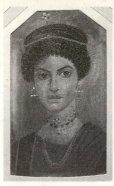

Define:
  encaustic

How does this work relate to Roman art? How does this work reflect its Egyptian origin?

DOMESTIC ART
AND ARCHITECTURE

7.50. Atrium of the House of the Vettii, Pompeii. 2d century BCE –79 CE. (page 214)

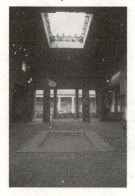

Define:
  atrium
  cubicula
  Tablinum
  insulae

7.51. August Mau's Four Styles of Pompeian wall painting. (page 214)

August Mau (1840–1909 produced what remains the scheme that underpins all stylistic analysis of Pompeian decor: he divided the wall painting into four 'Styles,' each representing a phase in the chronology of Pompeian painting, from the second century BCE to the final eruption in 79 CE.

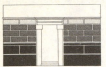

1. 'The First, or Incrustation, style': the wall is painted (and moulded in stucco) to imitate masonry blocks, no figured scenes. Second century BCE.

2. 'The Second, or Architectural, style': characteristically featuring illusionistic architectural vistas. c.100—15 BCE.

3. 'The Third, or Ornate, style': the vistas here give way to a delicate decorative scheme, concentrating on formal ornament. c.15 BCE.—50 CE.

4. 'The Fourth, or Intricate, style': a more extravagant painterly style, parading the whole range of decorative idioms. c.50 CE.

How does the quantity of surviving Roman domestic (mainly wall) painting compare to the quantity of surviving Greek painting?

7.52. First Style painting in the Samnite House, Herculaneum. Last 2d century BCE. (page 215)

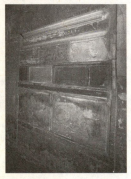

Why is this a good example of a First Style painting?

7.53. Second Style wall painting from The Villa of Mysteries, Pompeii. _Scenes of Dionysiac Mystery Cult_. ca. 60–50 BCE. (page 215)

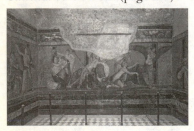

7.54. Second Style wall painting from the Villa of Publius Fannius Synistor at Boscoreale. Mid–1st century BCE. (page 216)

7.55. Wall painting of garden, from the Villa of Livia at Primaporta. ca. 20 BCE. (page 216)

How are 7.53., 7.54., and this work good examples of Second Style painting?

7.56. Third Style wall painting from Villa of Agrippa Postumus, Boscotrecase. ca. 10 BCE. (page 217)

Why is this a good example of Third Style painting?

7.57. Fourth Style wall painting, Ixion Room, House of Vettii, Pompeii. 63–79 CE. (page 217)

7.58. Still life painting of peaches and water jar, from Herculaneum. ca. 50 CE. (page 218)

Why are 7.57. and this still life good examples of Fourth Style painting?

THE LATE EMPIRE

7.59. Portrait of Philip the Arab. 244–249 CE. (page 219)

How does this portrait reflect the state of the Roman Empire at the time that it was carved?

7.60. Portrait group of the Tetrarchs. ca. 305 CE. (page 219)

How does this portrait group establish that each official is equal and the ultimate power remains in the hands of the emperor?

7.61. *Portrait of Constantine the Great.* Early 4th century CE. (page 220)

How does this work help establish the power and position of the Emperor? Is there anything about this work that might reflect Constantine's adherence to Christianity?

7.62. *Meleager Sarcophagus.* ca. 180 CE. (page 220)

What was the most popular subject matter for reliefs on sarcophagi during the second century CE?

7.63. Arch of Constantine, Rome. 312–315 CE. (page 221)

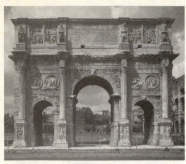

What is so unusual about the reliefs on this great monument?

7.64. Arch of Constantine, Rome. Schematic drawing showing reused sculpture (page 222)

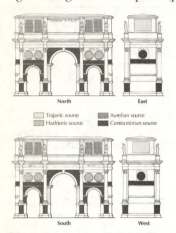

Define:
  spolia

7.65. Constantinian relief from Arch of Constantine, Rome. (page 223)

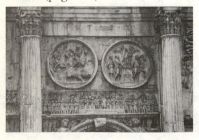

How do these reliefs indicate depth and recession?

7.66. Baths of Caracalla, Rome. ca. 211–216 CE. (page 224)

How were columns, architraves, and pediments used in the Baths of Caracalla?

7.67. Plan of Baths of Caracalla, Rome. ca. 211–216 CE. (page 224)

What activities took place in Roman baths such as this one?

7.68. Basilica Maxentius, renamed Basilica of Constantine. ca. 307 CE. (page 225)

What inspired the design of this great basilica?

7.69. Basilica of Maxentius, renamed Basilica of Constantine. Reconstructon. (page 225)

Why was this basilica re-named for Constantine?

LATE ROMAN ARCHITECTURE IN THE PROVINCES

7.70. Basilica, Lepcis Magna, Libya. Early 3rd century CE. (page 226)

Why was this basilica constructed in what is now Libya?

7.71. Palace of Diocletian, Spalato, Croatia. ca. 300 CE. (page 226)

7.72. Peristyle, Palace of Diocletian, Spalato Croatia. ca. 300 CE. (page 227)

Why was this palace designed the way it was?

7.73. Basilica of Constantine Chlorus, Trier, Germany. Early 4th century CE. (page 228)

7.74. Interior of Basilica of Constantius Chlorus, Trier, Germany. Early 4th century CE. (page 228)

How did the architect create the illusion that this Basilica is even larger than it is?

CHAPTER 8
Early Christian and Byzantine Art

Janson, pp. 234–275

The Christian religion was legalized in the Roman Empire by Constantine in 312 CE. This was a pivotal moment in Western history because within ten years Constantine had decided to move the seat of his power away from pagan Rome to the most Christianized part of the Western world, the Eastern Provinces. He built his new capital, Constantinople, virtually on top of the Greek city of Byzantium. Early Christian art is not so much a coherent style as it is a timeframe for works created prior to the split between the Western or Catholic Church and the Eastern Church. Byzantine defines the art, culture, and style of first the Eastern Roman Empire and then the Eastern Orthodox Church.

EARLY CHRISTIAN ART

NOTES

8.1. Painted ceiling. 4th century CE. (page 238)

Why are the paintings in the catacombs rather sketchy?

Why was an effort made to have a number of references to the Old Testament included in the catacomb paintings?

8.2. Sarcophagus. ca. 270 CE. (page 239)

Why did Early Christian sculpture avoid life-sized representations of the human figure?

8.3. Model of the Baptistery, the Christian Meeting House (*domus ecclesiae*) at Dura-Europos, Syria. Before. 256 CE. (page 241)

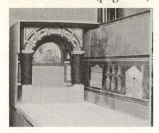

How does the art in the catacombs (8.1.) relate to the art in the Baptistery?

8.4. Plan of Old St. Peter's, Rome. ca. 324–400 CE. (page 242)

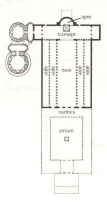

Define:
 apse
 clerestory
 transept
 martyrium
 nave
 baldachino
 narthex

8.5. Reconstruction of Old St. Peter's, Rome. ca. 400 (page 242)

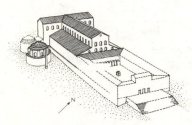

Why was the Roman basilica a suitable model for the Early Christian church?

What was the significance of the altar being placed at the eastern end of the nave?

8.6. Jacopo Grimaldi. *Interior of Old St. Peter's, Rome*. 1619 (page 243)

Why was Old St. Peter's constructed on the Vatican Hill?

8.7. Plan of Santa Costanza, Rome. ca. 350 CE. (page 243)

Define:
 ambulatory

How do central-plan churches relate to basilican churchs?

8.8. Interior, Santa Costanza, Rome. (page 243)

What is the significance of the cross in a funerary context?

How do Roman mausoleums relate to central-plan churches?

8.9. Reconstruction, Church of the Holy Sepulchre, Jerusalem. ca. 350 CE. (page 244)

Why did Constantine have the church of the Holy Sepulchre constructed?

8.10. Mausoleum of Galla Placidia, Ravenna. 425–450 CE. (page 245)

Define:
  Greek cross

Contrast the exterior with the interior of this structure and explain how the contrast in this and other Early Christian churches fits the idea of the ideal Christian?

8.11. Interior, Mausoleum of Galla Placidia, Ravenna. (page 246)

How do Early Christian mosaics relate to the illusionistic tradition of ancient painting?

8.12. *Good Shepherd*. Mausoleum of Galla Placidia, Ravenna. (page 247)

How is gold used in this mosaic?

8.13. Orthodox Baptistry, Ravenna. ca. 400–458 CE. (page 247)

What do the eight sides of the Orthodox Baptistry represent?

8.14. Dome mosaics, Orthodox Baptistry, Ravenna. ca. 458 (page 248)

Why was an image of Christ being baptized placed in the center of the dome?

8.15. Interior, Santa Maria Maggiore, Rome. ca. 432–440 CE. (page 248)

How does this church relate to Mary?

8.16. Triumphal arch. Santa Maria Maggiore, Rome. (page 249)

8.17. *The Parting of Lot and Abraham* and *Shepherds in a Landscape*. Santa Maria Maggiore, Rome. (page 249)

Relate the mosaics illustrated in 8.16. and 8.17. to the Roman reliefs on the Column of Trajan (7.28. and 7.29.).

8.18. Scenes from the Book of Kings, *Quedlinburg Itala*, ca. 425–450. (page 250)

Define:
  codex
  manuscript illumination
  parchment
  folio
  vellum
  scriptorium

8.19. Miniature from the *Vatican Vergil*. Early 5th century CE. (page 251)

What do the landscape and architectural elements in 8.18. and this illumination have to do with earlier Roman paintings?

8.20. *Sarcophagus of Junius Bassus*. Ca. 359 CE. (page 252)

How does this work show that the statues of Christianity had improved greatly by this time?

How does this work continue to reflect the Classical influence of the Greeks and the Romans?

BYZANTINE ART

8.21. Plan of San Vitale, Ravenna. 526–547 CE. (page 253)

Where do the greatest number of Byzantine monuments survive?

8.22. Section of San Vitale, Ravenna. (page 253)

clerestory

gallery

What aspects of San Vitale reflect influence from the Eastern Empire?

8.23. Exterior, San Vitale, Ravenna. (page 254)

When did domed, central-plan churchs begin to dominate Orthodox Christianity?

8.24. Interior (view from the apse), San Vitale, Ravenna. (page 254)

What does the placement of the narthex force visitors to do?

8.25. *Emperor Justinian and His Attendants*. ca. 547 CE. (page 255)

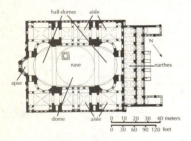

8.26. *Empress Theodora and Her Attendants*. ca. 547 CE. (page 255)

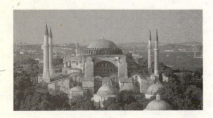

How do these mosaics of Justinian and Theodora reflect a new ideal of beauty and a new figure type?

8.27. Anthemius of Tralles and Isidorus of Miletus. Plan of Hagia Sophia, Istanbul. 532–537 CE. (page 256)

Who commissioned Hagia Sophia?

8.28. Exterior, Hagia Sophia, Istanbul. (page 256)

Compare Hagia Sophia with the Roman Pantheon.

8.29. Interior, Hagia Sophia, Istanbul (page 257)

What is the importance of light in the interior of Hagia Sophia?

8.30. Dome on pendentives. (page 259)

Define:
  pendentive

8.31. Arcade and capitals, Hagia Sophia, Istanbul. (page 259)

Compare the decoration of the structural members with their weight bearing function.

8.32. Interior (view from south aisle facing north-west), Hagia Sophia, Istanbul. (page 260)

Explain how Hagia Sophia combines aspects of a basilican church with aspects of a central plan church?

8.33. *Justinian as Conqueror*. ca. 525–550 CE.) (page 260)

What Roman sculpture inspired the portrait of Justinian?

8.34. *The Archangel Michael*. Early 6th century CE. (page 261)

How does this work relate to other works from Justinian's court such as religious architecture?

8.35. *Jacob Wrestling the Angel*, from the Vienna Genesis. Early 6th century CE. (page 262)

Define:
  continuous narration

8.36. *Christ*. 6th century CE. (page 263)

Define:
  icon

What was the function of an icon?

8.37. *Virgin and Child Enthroned Between Saints and Angels*. Late 6th century CE. (page 264)

How many influences are present in this icon?

8.38. *The Crucifixion and Iconoclasts*, from the *Khludov Psalter*. After 843 CE. (page 265)

Define:
   Iconoclastic Controversy
   Iconophiles
   Iconoclasts

What does the subject matter in this illumination mean?

8.39. Page with *Joshua and the Emissaries from Gibeon*, from the *Joshua Roll*. ca. 950 CE. (page 267)

Define:
   Second Golden Age

What is archaic about this work? Why was the work executed in such an impractical way?

8.40. *David Composing the Psalms*, from the *Paris Psalter*. ca. 950 CE. (page 267)

How does this work herald the revival of image-making after Iconoclasm?

8.41. *The Harbaville Triptych*. Late 10th century CE.

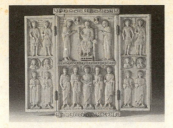

Define:
  deësis

8.42. *Christ Crowning Romanos and Eudokia*
("Romanos Ivory"). 945–949 CE. (page 269)

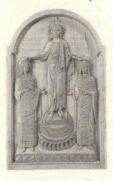

Describe the contrasts that exist within the figuration of both (8.41. and 8.42.) of these small scale ivory reliefs.

8.43. Plan of Church of the Dormition, 11th century CE. (page 269)

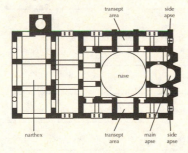

Describe the design of this Middle Byzantine church?

8.44. Interior (facing west), Church of the Dormition, Daphni, Greece. (page 269)

Define:
   squinches

What inspired the form of the dome?

8.45. Dome mosaics, Church of the Dormition, Daphni, Greece. (page 270)

Define:
   Christ Pantocrater

Taken together, what does the larger comprehensive mosaic program illustrate?

8.46. *The Cruxifixion*. Church of the Dormition, Daphni, Greece. (page 270)

What is the most important achievement of Middle Byzantine art?

8.47. St. Mark's (aerial view). Begun 1063 CE. (page 271)

What did the Venetians remain artistically dependent on?

8.48. Interior, St. Mark's, Venice. (page 271)

Define:
  lantern

How does the basic church design and its domes interrelate?

8.49. Interior, Cathedral. ca. 1180–1190 CE. Monreale, Italy. (page 272)

What is masterful about the last Byzantine mosaics executed, especially the Pantocrater?

8.50. *Madonna Enthroned.* Late 13th century. (page 272)

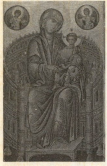

How did the Crusades impact Byzantine art as embodied by the *Madonna Enthroned* icon?

8.51. *Anastasis.* ca. 1310–1320 CE. (page 274)

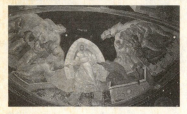

Define:
  Anastasis
  mandorla

Are the wall paintings in the mortuary chapel of Kariye Camii, especially the main scene of the *Anastsasis*, secondary to the mosaics?

CHAPTER 9
Islamic Art

Janson, pp. 276–309

Islamic art grew out of a synthesis of a number of sources including Graeco-Roman, Byzantine Christian, and Sasanian.

Islam became recognized as a major religious force in the early seventh century. Its birthplace was the Arabian peninsula, but within a century it had spread across Africa into Spain to the west and into present day Pakistan and Central Asia. The Islamic world was complex virtually from the beginning, with other cultures than the original Arab faithful joining the fold. Islamic art cannot be neatly described as a religious art even though religion plays a major role in Islamic culture. It included both religious and secular elements. It is no more or no less a reflection of that society and culture than any other art movement.

NOTES

THE FORMATION OF ISLAMIC ART

9.1. Page with kufic script from an Abbasid Qur'an, probably from Tunisia. 9th century. (page 279)

Define:
  kufic

Describe how important the art of beautiful writing and reverence for the word and the language of the word is to Islamic art.

9.2. The Dome of the Rock, Jerusalem. ca. 690 and later. (page 280)

What is especially significant about The Dome of the Rock?

9.3. Cutaway drawing, Dome of the Rock, Jerusalem. (page 281)

Describe the dome, the column, and their capitals and their meaning.

9.4. Interior, Dome of the Rock, Jerusalem. (page 281)

What visual vocalularies combine to create the decoration for the interior of the Dome of the Rock?

THE DEVELOPMENT OF ISLAMIC STYLE

9.5. Cutaway of a generic Arab hypostyle mosque. (page 282)

Define:
   minbar
   mosque
   mihrab
   qibla
   minaret
   dikka

What was the most important influence in the development of Islamic architecture? What did the architecture emphasize?

9.6. Floor fresco depicting two court musicians and a mounted hunter, from Qasr al-Hayr (West). ca. 730 (page 283)

What strongly influenced early Islamic secular architecture?

How does this floor fresco help illustrate this influence?

9.7. Aerial view of the Great Mosque of Kairouan, Tunisa. 8th century and later. (page 283)

Why are there so many entrances into this and most other mosques?

9.8. Interior of prayer hall, Great Mosque of Córdoba. (page 284)

Define:
   "horseshoe" arcade

What do the "horseshoe" arcades in the Great Mosque of Córdoba accomplish?

9.9. Carved stone grille on qibla wall of Great Mosque of Córdoba. Mid–10th century. (page 285)

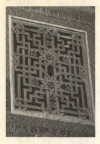

Define:
geometric arabesque

What secular additions were part of the Great Mosque of Córdoba?

What were institutions such as this often magnets for?

9.10. Ivory casket of al-Mughira, from Córdoba, ca. 960. (page 285)

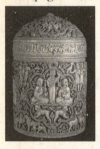

Why was this little casket and like objects created?

What does the imagery in this ivory casket incorporate?

ISLAMIC ART
AND THE PERSIAN INHERITANCE

9.11. Cutaway of a generic Persian four-iwan mosque. (page 286)

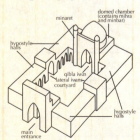

Define:
iwan
four-iwan mosque

What was the preferred building material throughout Iran and Islamic Central Asia?

9.12. Tomb of the Samanids, Bukhara, Uzbekistan. ca. 901. (page 286)

Define:
squinch

What is the basic concept of this small tomb?

How did Muhammad feel about the construction of tombs and shrines?

How did Muslim art and architecture affect Christian art and architecture after the Muslims were driven out of their European stronghold in Spain?

9.13. *Mina'i* dish with story of Bahram Gur and Azadeh from Iran. ca. 1200. (page 288)

Define:
luster
mina'i

Why do Iranian works of this period have strongly figural designs even though it is against strict Islamic dogma?

9.14. Muhammad ibn abd al-Wahid (caster) and
Masud ibn Ahmad al-Naggash (inlayer). 1163 CE.
(page 289)

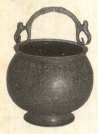

Where did the technique of inlaying precious metals into brass or bronze originate?

9.15. The al-Agmar Mosque, Cairo. ca. 1026
(page 290)

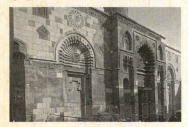

Define:
  muqarnas

What were the eleventh-century walls of Cairo
constructed out of?

9.16. Cloak of Roger II of Sicily. 12th century.
(page 290)

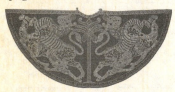

Where did much of the tradition of weaving
originate?

What other objects were produced by Fatimid
artists?

9.17. Detail of carved ivory frame with court scenes. Egypt. 12th century. (page 291)

What does this ornate carved ivory frame depict in contradiction of the Qur'an?

9.18. Yahya ibn Mahmud al-Wasiti. *Scene in an Arab Village*. ca. 1237. (page 291)

What does this work depict?

What did Ayyubid military architecture inspire? What arts flourished under the Ayyubids?

9.19. Sultan Han, Kayseri-Sivas Road, ca. 1229 Turkey. (page 292)

Artists and craftspeople from what cultures served the patronage of the Seljuk sultans?

Why was this complex constructed?

9.20. Tomb of Oljeytu, Sultaniya, Iran. ca. 1314
(page 293)

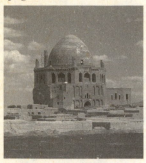

What is so unprecedented about this tomb?

9.21. Interior, Tomb of Oljeytu, Iran. (page 294)

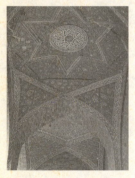

Whose enlightened patronage made this tomb
possible?

9.22. Madrasa of Ulugh Beg. ca. 1435. (page 294)

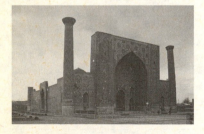

Define:
 madrasa

What about this building and other Timurid
buildings like it were never surpassed in the subse-
quent history of art in greater Iran?

Whose role led to the construction of this gigantic
congregational mosque?

9.23. Behzad. *A Poor Man Refused Admittance to a Mosque*. 1486 CE. (page 295)

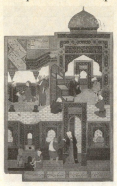

What did one of Timur's grandsons found and what did it serve as a central source for?

This work includes a series of legendary refinements to Islamic painting. What are they?

9.24. Madrasa–mosque-mausoleum complex of Sultan Hasan, Cairo. ca. 1354–1361. (page 296)

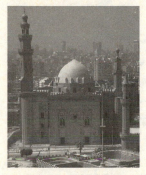

How did elaborate architecture under the Mamluks develop a new style? What was this new style?

9.25. Plan of the complex of Sultan Hasan, Cairo. (page 297)

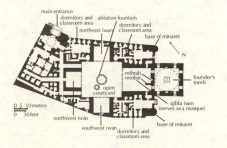

How was this great complex paid for?

9.26. Mosque lamp with blazon, from Cairo. ca. 1285. (page 297)

What is this work a strong representative of?

THE THREE LATE EMPIRES

9.27. Court of the Lions, Alhambra, Mid-14th century. Granada, Spain. (page 299)

What metaphors did this royal palace incorporate? What did the Alhambra influence?

9.28. Sinan the Architect. Cutaway of the mosque of Selim II (Selimiye), 1569–1574. Edirne, Turkey. (page 300)

What about this huge mosque proclaims the Ottoman architectural style?

9.29. Interior, Mosque of Selim II. (page 301)

How is the interior of the Mosque of Selim II different from the normal Arab hypostyle mosque and the Hagia Sophia?

What does the interior make a point of exposing?

9.30. Tile painted in hatayi style with saz design, by Shah Kulu. ca. 1525–1550. (page 302)

Define: saz
    hatayi

Is this a perfect example of the saz or hatayi design?

9.31. Sultan-Muhammad. *Allegory of Heavenly and Earthly Drunkenness*, from a Divan by Hafiz, from Tabriz. ca. 1529. (page 303)

What are the attributes of the new painting style of the Safvid period in Iran?

What great geniuses of Islamic art helped develop the new painting style?

9.32. Detail of the Sanguszko figural-design carpet, from Iran. ca. 1575–1600. (page 304)

What was the inspiration for the design of this rich carpet?

9.33. Aerial view of the mosque of Shah Abbas I (Masjid-i Shah), 1611–1616. Isfahan. (page 305)

Define:
  maidan

What was the maidan of the city of Isfahan oriented with? How was the mosque oriented?

9.34. Manohar and Abul Hasan. *Ceremonial Audience of Jahangir*, from a *Jahangir-nama* manuscript, northern India. ca. 1620. (page 306)

How are the people in this miniature Mughal painting executed?

What other unique qualities are present?

9.35. Wine cup of Shah Jahan, from northern India. Mid-17th century. (page 307)

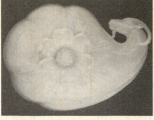

How does this wine cup illustrate the decorative arts under the Mughals in India?

9.36. The Taj Mahal, Agra, India. ca. 1650. (page 307)

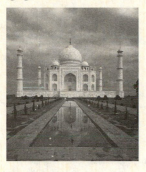

What influences can be seen in the design of the Taj Mahal?

What do the inscriptions on the walls of the Taj Mahal evoke?

CONTINUITY AND CHANGE IN ISLAMIC ART

CHAPTER 10
Early Medieval Art

Janson, pp. 310–343

The phrase "the Dark Ages" has been mistakenly attached to the period in Western Europe that falls between the fall of Rome (476 CE) and the eleventh century. This period was actually a time of unparalleled cultural activity.

The blending of the surface decoration and the portable arts of the Sasanians, the Celts, the Germanic tribes, and the Scandinavian peoples joined with the arts, philosophy, and religion of the Early Christians to create a true cultural revitalization of Europe.

The 7th and 8th centuries brought the blossoming of the art of the Irish monasteries. Charlemagne, beginning in 768, brought the revival of the best of the politics and culture of the Roman Empire, and under the 10th-century Ottonian kings, German art and architecture became dominant.

NOTES

ANGLO-SAXON AND VIKING ART

10.1. Golden buckle, from the Sutton Hoo ship burial. First half of 7th century. (page 314)

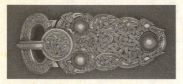

How does the design of Germanic and Celtic works differ from Greek and Roman works?

Define:
 animal style
 horror vacui
 inlaid neillo
 cloisonné

10.2. Hinged clasps, from Sutton Hoo ship burial. First half of 7th century. (page 314)

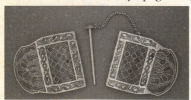

What appears to be the principal medium used to create "animal style" works? Is this medium particularly characteristic of the culture that utilized it?

Why was gold so important during the Middle Ages?

10.3. Purse cover, from the Sutton Hoo ship burial. First half of 7th century. (page 315)

What design element on this purse cover reminds of ancient Mesopotamia?

What different influences or cultural interchanges are evident in the works found at the Sutton Hoo ship burial (10.1., 10.2. and 10.3.)?

10.4. *Animal Head*, from the Oseberg ship burial. ca. 834 CE. (page 316)

How can this work be related to the objects found at Sutton Hoo?

HIBERNO-SAXON ART

10.5. *Symbol of Saint Matthew*, from the *Book of Durrow*. ca. 680 CE. (page 317)

How do the ornamental patterns in this illumination recall the objects from Sutton Hoo?

Monasteries in what country were true centers of learning and the arts? What styles combined to create their unique images?

10.6. Cross page, from the *Lindisfarne Gospels*. ca. 700 CE. (page 318)

Define:
  colophon

In this illumination how are organic and geometric shapes treated?

Compare this Cross page with the Golden Buckle (10.1.) from Sutton Hoo and the Animal Head (10.4.) from the Oseberg ship burial.

10.7. *St. Matthew*, from the *Lindisfarne Gospels*. ca. 700 CE. (page 319)

How does the illumination of St. Matthew from the *Lindisfarne Gospels* differ from the illumination of Saint Matthew from the *Book of Durrow*?

10.8. *Ezra Restoring the Bible*, from the *Codex Amiatinus*. Early 8th century. (page 319)

Could the figure of St. Matthew (10.7.) and the figure of Ezra be from the same source? Why are the two illuminations executed so differently?

10.9. Chi Rho Iota page, from *Book of Matthew* (1:18), from the *Book of Kells*. ca. 800 CE. (page 320)

While there is a great deal about the Chi Rho Iota page that reminds of the Cross page (10.6.), the *Tara Brooch* (page 313), and the Sutton Hoo works (10.1., 10.2. and 10.3.) how does it differ?

How did Irish monks influence medieval civilization for several hundred years?

CAROLINGIAN ART

10.10. *Equestrian Statue of a Carolingian Ruler* (Charles the Bald?). 9th century. (page 321)

What probably influenced this work? Why would Charles the Bald have been portrayed this way?

10.11. *Christ Enthroned,* from the *Godescalc Gospels (Lectionary)*. 781–783 CE. (page 322)

What does this work generally reflect?

How did Charlemagne promote learning and culture?

10.12. *St. Matthew*, from the *Gospel Book of Charlemagne (Coronation Gospels)*. ca. 800–810 CE. (page 322)

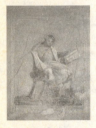

How was the *Gospel Book of Charlemagne* used by later German emperors?

Why do some scholars claim the artist of this work must have come from Byzantium or Italy?

10.13. *Portrait of Menander*. ca. 70 CE. (page 323)

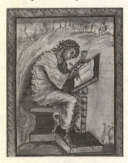

Can comparing this work from Pompeii to *St. Matthew* (10.12.) help in understanding how much the artist of *St. Matthew* knows about the Roman painting style?

10.14. *St. Matthew*, from the *Gospel Book of Archbishop Ebbo of Reims*. 816–835 CE. (page 323)

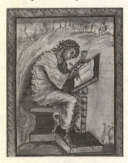

Discuss how this work compares to the other illuminations of St. Matthew in the text (10.5., 10.7., 10.8. and 10.12). How has the depiction of the evangelist changed?

10.15. Illustrations to Psalms 43 and 44, from the *Utrecht Psalter*. ca. 820–832 CE. (page 324)

What work from ancient Rome is recalled by this illustration? What quality of draftsmanship has not been present in earlier works?

10.16. Front cover of binding, *Lindau Gospels*. ca. 870 CE. (page 325)

Define:
   turret

What metalwork tradition was adapted to the Carolingian revival of the Roman Empire?

10.17. Odo of Metz. Interior of the Palace Chapel of Charlemagne, 792–805 CE. (page 326)

Define:
   westwork
   tribune

10.18. Section of the Palace Chapel of Charlemagne. (page 327)

What was Charlemagne's palace complex modeled after?

How does the Palace Chapel compare to its probable inspiration the Church of San Vitale in Ravenna (8.21., 8.22., 8.23. and 8.24.)?

10.19. Abbey Church of Saint-Riquier, Monastery of Centula, France. Dedicated ca. 790. (page 327)

Define:
  cloister

What was symbolic about the shape of the cloister of this monastery?

What was the significance of the westwork of the church of Saint-Riquier?

10.20. Westwork, Abbey Church. Late 9th century CE, with later additions. Corvey, Germany. (page 328)

What is so impressive about this westwork?

10.21. Plan of a monastery. Redrawn, with inscriptions translated into English from the Latin, from the original of ca. 820 CE. (page 329)

What features confirm that a medieval monastery was a complex, self-contained unit?

OTTONIAN ART

10.22. Interior, looking east, Church of St. Cyriakus. Founded 961 CE. Gernrode, Germany. (page 331)

What basic church form did the Church of St. Cyriakus follow?

What was added that wasn't present before?

What was the new emphasis as a result of this addition?

10.23. Reconstructed plan. Abbey Church of St. Michael's. 1001–1033 CE. Hildesheim, Germany. (page 332)

What church was the inspiration for the Abbey Church of St. Michael's? What other church does it recall?

10.24. Exterior, Abbey Church of St. Michael's. Hildesheim, Germany. (page 332)

How does St. Michael's carry symmetry further than earlier churches?

How did the architect achieve a harmonious balance between the longitudinal and horizontal axes throughout the structure?

10.25. Interior, with view toward the apse, Abbey Church of St. Michael's. Hildesheim, Germany. (page 333)

Why did the architect raise the floor of the church above the level of the rest of the church?

Why was Bishop Bernward of Hildesheim considered the most ambitious patron of art and architecture in the Ottonian age?

10.26. Doors of Bishop Bernward, Hildesheim Cathedral (originally made for Abbey Church of St. Michael's, Hildesheim). 1015 CE. (page 334)

Where did the idea for these doors probably originate?

10.27. Schematic diagram of the scenes on the Doors of Bishop Bernward. (page 335)

Old Testament	Comparison of themes	New Testament
Formation of Eve	Paradise Lost and then Paradise Gained	Noli Me Tangere
Eve Presented to Adam	Salutations	The Three Marys at the Tomb
Temptation and Fall	Tree of Knowledge (sin) vs. Tree of Life (The Cross, Salvation)	The Crucifixion
Accusation and Judgment of Adam and Eve	Judgment	Judgment of Jesus by Pilate
Expulsion from Paradise	Separation from God vs. Reunion with God	Presentation of Jesus in Temple
Adam and Eve Working	Firstborn Sons of Eve (Cain) and Mary (Jesus); Poverty vs. Wealth	Adoration of the Magi
Offerings by Cain (grain) and Abel (lamb)	Abel's Sacrificial Lamb vs. Jesus, Lamb of God	The Nativity
Cain Slaying Abel	Despair, Sin, Murder vs. Hope and Everlasting Life	The Annunciation

Many scholars consider the doors to have created several firsts. What were these firsts?

What tells us how important these doors were in their own time?

10.28. *Accusation and Judgment of Adam and Eve,* from the Doors of Bishop Bernward. (page 336)

What was the basic subject matter of the left door and the right door?

10.29. *Temptation and Fall,* from the Doors of Bishop Bernward. (page 336)

What role does Eve play in these doors and during the Ottonian period as a whole?

10.30. Column of Bishop Bernward, Hildesheim Cathedral (originally made for Abbey Church of St. Michael's). 1015–1022 CE. (page 337)

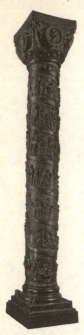

This column with spiraling reliefs depicting Jesus' life is a strong reminder of what Roman structure? What was Bishop Bernward trying to do with all of his visual references to ancient Rome?

10.31. *Christ Blessing Emperor Otto II and Empress Theophano.* 982–983 CE. (page 338)

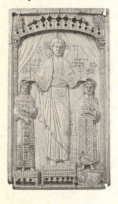

How is the king portrayed in this ivory?

10.32. *Otto III Receiving the Homage of the Four Parts of the Empire* and *Otto III Between Church and State*, from the *Gospel Book of Otto III*. ca. 1000 CE. (page 339)

The imperial grandeur of the *Gospel Book of Otto III* equals what other work? Otto is presented in this manuscript as the rightful and worthy heir of what historical figures?

10.33. *Jesus Washing the Feet of St. Peter*, from the *Gospel Book of Otto III*. ca. 1000 CE. (page 339)

How is Christ's depiction different from the way he was portrayed in Early Christian works?

10.34. *St. Luke*, from the *Gospel Book of Otto III*. ca. 1000 CE. (page 340)

How is the depiction of St. Luke different than the earlier depictions of evangelists in Hiberno-Saxon and Carolingian manuscripts (10.7., 10.8., 10.12. and 10.14.)?

10.35. The *Gero Crucifix*. ca. 970 CE. (page 341)

Define:
  reliquary

What is new about the scale of this work?

What did the sculptor transform the *Gero Crucifix* into?

10.36. *Virgin of Essen*. ca. 980 CE. (page 342)

How was the *Virgin of Essen* a first?

What does the apple in her hand symbolize? What is the sculpture conceptually related to?

CHAPTER 11
ROMANESQUE ART

Janson, pp. 344–383

The eleventh and twelfth centuries are known as the Romanesque period because Roman architecture and art, because of the continuing appeal of its ancient but enduring monuments, was embraced as a model as never before. Manuscript illuminations, metalwork, and ivory carvings created since Medieval times continued to be crafted, but the revival of monumental architecture and sculpture, along with the beginnings of an economic, cultural and social revolution, distinguished the period.

Because of the Christian Crusades waged between 1095 and the fourth final Crusade, which ended with the fall of Constantinople in 1204, huge numbers of people made pilgrimages to sacred sites and to visit relics housed in the ever increasing Roman-appearing churches. These churches were larger and more richly decorated than those of the early Middle Ages.

NOTES

FIRST EXPRESSIONS OF ROMANESQUE STYLE

11.1. Nave and choir (looking east), Sant Vincenç. ca 1029–1040. (page 348)

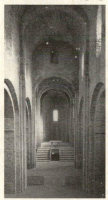

Define:
  bay
  Chancel
  compound piers

How is Sant Vincenç an excellent example of an early phase of Romanesque architecture?

Sant Vincenç uses a major architectural innovation of the Romanesque period. What was this innovation?

11.2. Lintel of west portal, Saint-Genis-des-Fontaines, France. 1020–1021. (page 349)

In what way is this lintel a sculptural innovation? What were the major influences on this sculpture?

MATURE ROMANESQUE

11.3. Plan of Cathedral of Santiago de Compostela, Spain (after Dehio). (page 351)

Define:

      apsidioles
      pilgrimage plan church
      colonnettes

What was Santiago de Compostelas' solution to visitors being able to move around the church in a seamless fashion?

11.4. Nave, Santiago de Compostela, Spain. ca. 1075–1120. (page 351)

How did the author of the *Pilgrim's Guide* to the church (written around 1130) liken the churchs' building material to that of the Roman past?

11.5. Reliquary casket with symbols of the four Evangelists. ca. 1150. (page 352)

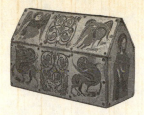

Identify:
reliquary
champlevé

Why would one be reminded of migration and early medieval metalwork when looking at this reliquary?

11.6. Plan of Saint-Sernin, Toulouse. ca. 1070–1120. France (after Conant). (page 353)

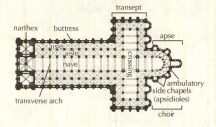

How is Saint-Sernin different from Santiago de Compostela?

What structure possibly influenced the design of Saint-Sernin?

11.7. Saint-Sernin, Toulouse (aerial view). (page 353)

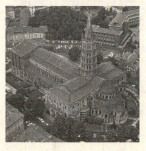

How did the roof levels affect the exterior appearance of the church?

11.8. Nave and choir, Saint-Sernin, Toulouse.
(page 353)

Saint-Sernin recaptures the look of ancient Roman
architecture in virtually every respect but it is different
in at least one important way. What is this difference?
What are the two major reasons that the ceiling is
vaulted stone instead of flat wood?

11.9. *Christ in Majesty (Maiestas Domini).* ca. 1096.
Saint-Sernin, Toulouse. (page 354)

What does the shallow relief and many decorative
effects of this plaque recall?

What specific effect might the image of Christ in the
Godescale Gospels (10.11.) have had on this plaque?

What might have been the primary reason for the
re-introduction of large-scale sculpture?

11.10. Gunzo and others. Plan of Monastery of Cluny (Cluny III), France (after Conant). ca. 1088–1130. (page 355)

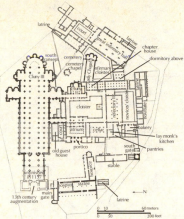

Which Benedictine order was probably the most important as far as the development of Romanesque art?

What was the largest Romanesque church ever built?

11.11. Reconstruction of Abbey Church of Cluny (Cluny III), from east. (after Conant). (page 356)

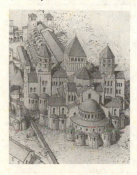

What were the proportions for Cluny III based on?

11.12. Reconstruction of Abbey Church of Cluny (Cluny III), nave and interior. (after Conant). (page 357)

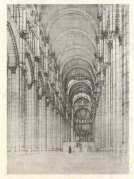

Define:
  triforium

How did the stone vault of Cluny III and other Romanesque churches affect musical performances?

How were the arches in the nave arcade altered? What very positive result comes from this alteration?

11.13. Cloister, Priory of Saint–Pierre. ca. 1100. Moissac, France. (page 357)

Why was St. Bernard of Clairvaux so upset about the cloister sculpture of Saint-Pierre at Moissac?

11.14. South portal with *Second Coming of Christ* on tympanum, Church of Saint-Pierre, Moissac. ca. 1115–1130. (page 357)

What is the sculptural subject of this Romanesque portal? How does the present abstraction relate to earlier medieval art?

11.15. Romanesque portal ensemble. (page 359)

Define:
  typanum
  trumeau
  jamb
  spandrel

What part or parts of this portal are modeled after Islamic devices? What were Christians saying about Arab artistic achievements?

11.16. Trumeau and jambs, south portal, Church of Saint-Pierre, Moissac. (page 360)

Compare the crossed lions on this trumeau, the interlaced animals and shapes found in the metalwork from the Sutton Hoo ship burial (10.1., 10.2. and 10.3.) as well as Hiberno-Saxon illuminations (10.6. and 10.9.). Where do these heraldic animals ultimately descend from?

Why were savage or monstrous animals and creatures included in the iconography of Romanesque art and architecture?

11.17. East flank, south portal, Church of Saint-Pierre, Moissac. (page 360)

What is meant by saying that the visual messages at Moissac are didactic?

11.18. West portal, with *Last Judgment* by Gislebertus on tympanum, Cathedral of Saint-Lazare. ca. 1120–1135. (page 361)

Define:
    archivolt

Who is the sculptor credited with creating the sculpture at the Cathedral of Saint-Lazare?

Why is the tympanum of the west portal an extremely good example of a Romanesque scene of the *Last Judgment*? Why was a scene of the *Last Judgment* a standard Romanesque typanum subject?

11.19. Gislebertus, *Eve*, right half of lintel, north portal from Cathedral of Saint-Lazare, Autun. Musée Rolin, Autun. (page 362)

What does *Eve's* pose emulate?

11.20. *Sarcophagus of Doña Sancha*, front and back sides. ca. 1120. Monastério de las Benedictinas, Jaca, Spain. (page 363)

What antique tradition does the right panel of the front of the *Sarcophagus of Doña Sancha* rely on?

Why is the center group on the front side of the sarcophagus the only one not covered by an arch?

What does this sarcophagus help tell us about the role of women in eleventh- and twelfth-century Spain?

11.21. *Christ and Apostles*. Painting in the apse. Early 12th century. Priory of Berzé-la-Ville, France. (page 364)

What probably influenced the proportions of the figures in the wall paintings at the Priory of Berzé-la-Ville and the lost wall paintings at Cluny III?

11.22. Plan of Fontenay Abbey, France. (page 365)

Compare the plan of the Abbey Church at Fontenay with the plan of the Carolingian Monastery of St. Gall (10.21.) and the plan of the Monastery of Cluny (11.10.). Which other plan does the Abbey Church at Fontenay most closely emulate?

11.23. Nave, Abbey Church, Fontenay, 1139–1147. (page 365)

Why did this church lack any applied decoration including painting and sculpture?

11.24. Choir ca. 1060–1075 and nave ca. 1095–1115. Saint-Savin-sur-Gartempe, France. (page 366)

Define:
  hall church

11.25. *The Building of the Tower of Babel*. Early 12th century. Detail of painting on the nave vault, Saint-Savin-sur-Gartempe, France. (page 366)

What was Saint-Savin-sur-Gartempe designed particularly to offer?

11.26. *Pentecost*, from the *Cluny Lectionary*. Early 12th century. (page 367)

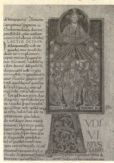

What accounts for the consistency in manuscript style from northern France to southern England?

What are the different reasons that St. Peter is in the central location in this illumination?

11.27. *St. Matthew*, from the *Codex Colbertinus*. ca. 1100. (page 367)

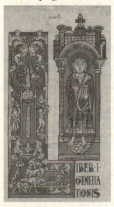

Why does the image of St. Matthew remind of the pier reliefs from the Moissac cloister?

What visual devices are still reminiscent of the early Middle Ages?

11.28. *St. Mark*, from a Gospel Book produced at the Abbey at Corbie. Early 12th century. (page 369)

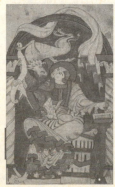

What visual element has disappeared?

What three visual elements are fully integrated in this illumination?

11.29. *Initial I*, from Gregory the Great's *Moralia in Job*.1111. (page 370)

Why was the artist of this Cistercian illumination allowed to include naturalistic elements in addition to the normal nonfigurative initials?

11.30. *St. John the Evangelist*, from the *Gospel Book of Abbot Wedricus*. ca. 1147 (page 370)

What is the ultimate source of the inspiration for this illumination?

REGIONAL VARIANTS
OF ROMANESQUE STYLE

11.31. West façade, Notre-Dame-la-Grande, Early 12th Century. Poitiers, France. (page 371)

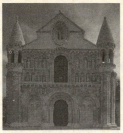

Define:
  gable

What does the broad screen-like façade of the front of Notre-Dame-la-Grande offer?

11.32. West façade, Saint-Gilles-du-Gard, France. Mid-12th century. (page 372)

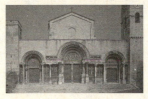

What was the inspiration for the façade of Saint-Gilles-du-Gard?

What would the depiction of Jesus' entry into Jerusalem on the lintel supporting the left tympanum have meant to townspeople of the time?

11.33. Baptistery, Cathedral, and Campanile (view from the west). 1053–1272, Pisa, Italy. (page 372)

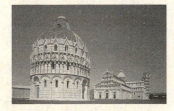

Define:
  campanile
  latin cross

What is the Italian tradition for the use of towers in churches?

What was the main inspiration for the Italian baptistery?

11.34. Interior, Pisa Cathedral. (page 373)

The interior of Pisa Cathedral has somewhat taller proportions than what? How was the roof different than most Romanesque churches outside of Italy?

11.35. Baptistery of San Giovanni. ca. 1060–1150. Florence, Italy. (page 374)

Romanesque Tuscan architecture used a deliberate revival of what Roman practice?

How is the Baptistery of San Giovanni related to the Orthodox Baptistery in Ravenna (8.13., 8.14.)?

11.36. Façade, San Miniato al Monte, 1062–1150. Florence, Italy. (page 374)

How do the individual additive units decorating Florentine Romanesque buildings parallel pilgrimage churches and French Romanesque portals?

11.37. Renier of Huy. Baptismal Font. 1107–1118. Saint-Barthélemy, Liège Belgium. (page 375)

What did Christian writers say Solomon's basin was a protype for and the twelve oxen were a precursor to?

Why did Mosan sculptures produce Classical forms?

11.38. Reconstruction of interior of Speyer Cathedral, Germany. ca. 1030–1061. (after Conant) (page 376)

11.39. Interior, Speyer Cathedral. ca. 1030–1061; vaulted ca. 1080–1106. (page 376)

How did Speyer Cathedral use groin vaults? How does the scale of Speyer Cathedral compare to other churches of the period?

11.40. *Crowds Gaze in Awe at a Comet as Harold Is Told of an Omen*. Detail of the *Bayeux Tapestry*. ca. 1066–1183. (page 377)

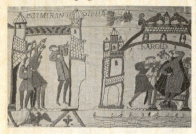

What is this work in actuality? What do the scenes record?

11.41. *The Battle of Hastings*. Detail of the *Bayeux Tapestry*. (page 377)

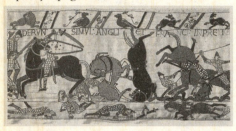

How are the *Bayeaux Tapestry* and the *Gospel Book of Abbot Wedricus* related?

Review and define:

arcuation	quadrant vault
barrel vault	ribbed vault
centering	springing
diagonal rib	thrust
dome	transverse rib
groin vault	web

11.42. Plan of Durham Cathedral, England. 1093–1130. (after Conant) (page 379)

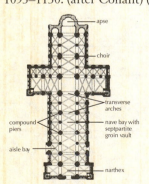

How was Durham Cathedral an advance beyond Speyer Cathedral?

11.43. Nave (looking east), Durham Cathedral. (page 380)

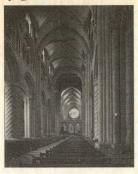

How were the odd-numbered piers constructed compared to the way the even-numbered piers were? How is this different than Speyer Cathedral?

11.44. Transverse section of Durham Cathedral (after Acland) (page 380)

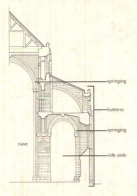

How were buttresses used in Durham Cathedral? Was this a well-established practice?

11.45. Plan of Saint-Étienne. Begun 1068. Caen, France. (page 381)

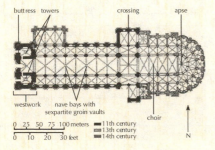

Who founded the abbey church of Saint-Étienne at Caen?

11.46. West façade, Saint-Étienne. Caen, France. (page 381)

What does the west work of Saint-Étienne proclaim itself to be?

11.47. Nave, Saint-Étienne. Vaulted ca. 1115–1120. Caen, France. (page 381)

How is the ribbing of the groined nave vaults of Saint-Étienne and Durham Cathedral different? How then does the nave of Saint-Étienne compare to the nave of Durham Cathedral?

THE PARADOXICAL MEANING OF ROMANESQUE

11.48. *Mouth of Hell*, from the *Winchester Psalter*. ca. 1150. From Winchester, England. (page 382)

What does the *Mouth of Hell* from the *Winchester Psalter* say about the hopes and fears of those living in Europe during the twelfth century?

CHAPTER 12
GOTHIC ART

Janson, pp. 384–431

Beginning about 1140 in the province of the Île-de-France, Gothic art spread across France and then across virtually all of Europe and England. It was first identified as *opus modernum* (modern work) or *opus francigenum* (French work) because its roots were in a tiny area around Paris. Within one hundred years most of Europe had adopted the style which was to become known as Gothic in the sixteenth century.

The style was first identified in one of the last great abbey churches, Saint-Denis. Architecture was the initial vehicle that drove the expansion of the Gothic style, but significant successes followed in the areas of sculpture and painting.

The year 1400 saw the Gothic visual impact lessen. Italy was no longer included and by 1550 only England continued to use elements of the Gothic style.

EARLY GOTHIC ART IN FRANCE

12.1. Plan of the choir and ambulatory, Abbey Church of Saint-Denis, France. 1140–1144. (page 387)

apsidal chapels
ambulatory
apse
choir

Identify:
  Abbot Suger

What was the psychological and political importance of Saint-Denis?

How is the plan of the choir different from earlier churches?

NOTES

161

12.2. Ambulatory, Abbey Church of Saint-Denis. (page 389)

Define:
  harmony
  respond

What most distinguished the interior of Saint-Denis?

What did the term *architect* mean to people during Medieval times?

12.3. West facade, Abbey Church of Saint-Denis. ca. 1137–1140. (page 391)

What basic features do Saint-Denis and Saint Étienne (11.45., 11.46. and 11.47.) share? What are the important differences?

Where do you have to look to be able to imagine what the sculpture on the west facade of Saint-Denis looked like?

12.4. West facade, Cathedral of Notre-Dame. Chartres, France. ca. 1145–1220. (page 392)

Define:
   spire

In what way is the west facade of Notre-Dame, Chartres reminiscent of Saint-Denis?

12.5. West portal (Royal Portal), Cathedral of Notre-Dame, Chartres. ca. 1145 – 1150. (page 392)

Why is it possible to say that the sculpture on the west portal of Notre-Dame, Chartres appears to be reacting against the horrifying images from Romanesque art and architecture?

12.6. Jamb statues, west portal, Cathedral of Notre-Dame, Chartres. (page 393)

What is fundamentally revolutionary about the jamb figures of Notre-Dame, Chartres?

12.7. Nave, Cathedral of Notre-Dame, Laon, France. ca. 1160–1210. (page 394)

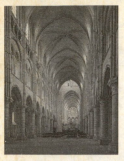

What is included in the interior elevation of Notre-Dame, Laon that makes it an ideal example of early Gothic church architecture?

12.8. Plan, Cathedral of Notre-Dame, Paris. ca. 1155–ca. 1250. (page 394)

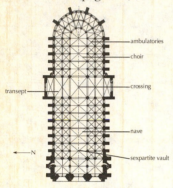

What is stressed in both the plan and the elevation of Notre-Dame, Paris?

12.9. Nave, Cathedral of Notre-Dame, Paris. (page 395)

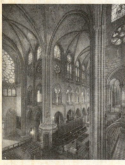

What did design changes reveal about what the builders hoped to achieve?

12.10. West facade, Cathedral of Notre-Dame, Paris. ca. 1200–1250. (page 396)

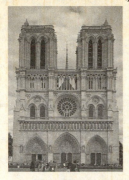

What is the most monumental aspect of the exterior of Notre-Dame, Paris?

What is even more apparent than at Saint-Denis?

HIGH GOTHIC ART IN FRANCE

12.11. Plan, Cathedral of Notre-Dame (as rebuilt after 1194), Chartres. (page 396)

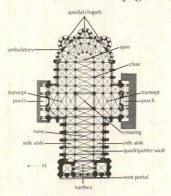

What is Notre-Dame, Chartres' most important possession?

How did civic and ecclesiastical authorities turn the negative aspects of the devastating fire of 1194 into a positive?

12.12. Nave and choir, Cathedral of Notre-Dame, Chartres. ca. 1194–1220. (page 397)

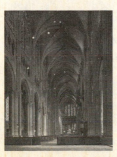

Define:
    liminal or transitional zone

How did the builders accent the significance of entering the building?

What was the first masterpiece of High Gothic style?

The consistent use of what feature helps add to the height of Notre-Dame, Chartres and other Gothic cathedrals?

12.13. Axonometric projection of a High Gothic cathedral (after Acland). (page 397)

What was eliminated in order to impose a three-part elevation on the wall?

12.14. (a) Sexpartite vaulting and (b) quadripartite vaulting. (page 398)

Define:
    quadripartite vault
    sexpartite vault

What did a builder no longer have to worry about when quadripartite vaults replaced sexpartite vaults?

12.15. Cathedral of Notre-Dame, Chartres (from the south) (page 398)

12.16. Transverse section of Cathedral of Notre-Dame, Chartres (after Acland). (page 399)

Define:
  flying buttress

12.17. Flying buttresses, Cathedral of Notre-Dame, Chartres. (page 399)

Define:
  freemason
  freestone
  roughmasons

What were the flying buttresses (12.15. and 12.16.) extensively used in Notre-Dame, Chartres and Paris designed to accomplish?

12.18. North transept, Cathedral of Notre-Dame, Chartres. (page 400)

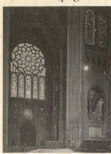

Define:
  rose window

How can stained glass relate to arts and crafts from the Middle Ages?

Whose methods were utilized when glass workers began to create huge stained-glass windows?

12.19. *Notre Dame de la Belle Verrière*. ca. 1170. (framing panels are 13th century). (page 401)

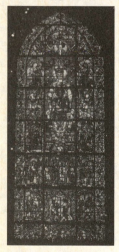

Define:
  bar tracery
  lancets
  plate tracery

What kind of system was used to help design Gothic architecture including stained glass?

12.20. Villard de Honnecourt. *Wheel of Fortune*. ca. 1240. (page 402)

12.21. Villard de Honnecourt. *Front View of a Lion*. ca. 1240. (page 402)

Did Villard de Honnecourt use the same design system used by architects, stonemasons, and glass workers?

12.22. Portals, north transept, Cathedral of Notre-Dame, Chartres. ca. 1204–1230. (page 404)

Define:
  Mariology

Who was the north transept devoted to?

Notre-Dame, Chartres is just one Gothic church to be named after the Virgin. Name several others.

12.23. *Coronation of the Virgin* (tympanum), *Dormition and Assumption of the Virgin* (lintel), north portal, Cathedral of Notre-Dame, Chartres. ca. 1210. (page 404)

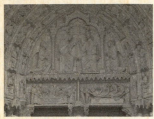

How is this representation of the Virgin, in this case, a Western invention rather than the previously prevailing Byzantine model?

12.24. Jamb statues, south transept portal, Cathedral of Notre-Dame, Chartres. ca. 1215–1220. Left-most figure (St. Theodore) ca. 1230. (page 405)

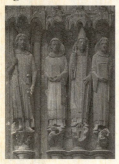

How is the jamb figure of St. Theodore an excellent example of the move away from the elongated, cylindrical shape of Early Gothic examples?

12.25. Robert de Luzarches, Thomas de Cormont, and Renaud de Cormont. Plan, Cathedral of Notre-Dame, Amiens. Begun 1220. (page 405)

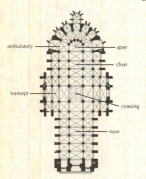

Why is it said that the High Gothic style reached its climax with Notre-Dame, Amiens?

What indicates that the social status of the architects of Notre-Dame, Amiens was higher than previous architects?

12.26. Nave and side aisle, Cathedral of Notre-Dame, Amiens. (page 406)

Why is the nave elevation and width of Notre-Dame, Amiens considered the dominant achievement of High Gothic style technically and aesthetically?

12.27. Comparison of nave elevations in same scale (after Grodecki). (page 406)

Notre-Dame, Paris   Chartres Cathedral   Amiens Cathedral

Compare the nave elevation and width of these three cathedrals. What does it say about the way cathedrals developed from the Early Gothic to the High Gothic. Why were these changes made?

12.28. Plan, Cathedral of Notre-Dame, Reims. ca. 1225–1290. (page 407)

ambulatory
apse
choir
transept
crossing

nave

How is it possible to tell how closely related Notre-Dame, Reims and Notre-Dame, Paris are to each other?

12.29. Cathedral of Notre-Dame, Reims (from the west). (page 407)

Define:
  pinnacles

Trace the development of the Gothic style cathedral west front by comparing Notre-Dame, Paris with the High Gothic Notre-Dame, Reims.

12.30. *Annunciation* and *Visitation*, west portal, Cathedral of Notre-Dame, Reims. ca. 1230–1265. (page 408)

Compare the *Visitation* figures from the west portal of Notre-Dame, Reims to St. Theodore from Chartres. How have the *Visitation* figures moved beyond even St. Theodore?

Note: In general conversation Notre-Dame, Paris is the only Gothic Cathedral consistently addressed as Notre-Dame. To avoid confusion Notre-Dame, Chartres, Notre-Dame, Amiens, Notre-Dame, Laon, and Notre-Dame, Reims are often identified as Chartres, Amiens, Laon, and Reims.

12.31. *Melchizedek and Abraham*, interior west wall, Cathedral of Notre-Dame, Reims. ca. 1260–1270. (page 409)

Define:
  "elegant style"

How are the concerns of the sculptor of *Melchizedek and Abraham* pictorial as well as sculptural?

12.32. *Signs of the Zodiac* (Leo, Virgo and Libra) and *Labors of the Months* (July, August and September), west facade, Amiens Cathedral. ca. 1220–1230. (page 409)

Define:
  quatrefoil

How do these quartrfoil reliefs from Amiens show growth beyond the same subjects on Romanesque and early Gothic portals?

12.33. Sainte-Chapelle, Paris (from the southwest). 1241–1248. (Rose window, late 15th century. (page 410)

Identify: King Louis IX (Saint Louis).

What did King Louis IX accomplish in a political and artistic sense?

What compelled Louis IX to construct Sainte-Chapelle? What was an early prototype for Sainte-Chapelle?

12.34 Interior of upper chapel, Sainte-Chapelle. (page 411)

What does the structure actually function as?

What is the most important feature of Sainte-Chapelle?

How did the builders compensate for keeping the buttresses very close to the building so they wouldn't cast shadows across the windows?

12.35. Saint-Urbain, Begun 1262. Troyes, France. (page 412)

What is eliminated from the elevation of Saint-Urbain? What does the deletion accomplish?

12.36. Interior, Saint-Urbain, Troyes. (page 413)

What does the architectural ornamentation of Saint-Urbain, Troyes tell us about the state of Gothic cathedrals?

12.37. *Crucifixion and Deposition*, from the *Psalter of Blanche of Castile*. ca. 1230. (page 413)

Define:
   Blanche of Castile
   court style
   rayonnant

What does *Crucifixion and Deposition* from the *Psalter of Blanche of Castile* remind of?

12.38. *Scenes from the Apocalypse*, from a *Bible moralisée*. ca. 1225–1235. (page 414)

Define:
  moralized Bible (*Bible moralisée*)

Why were works such as this created? What are the vertically stacked roundels reminiscent of?

12.39. *Nahash the Ammonite Threatening the Jews at Jabesh*, from the *Psalter of St. Louis*. 1253–1270. (page 414)

Why does this work remind so strongly of the architecture and stained glass of Sainte-Chapelle, Chartres and Reims?

LATE GOTHIC ART IN FRANCE

12.40. Master Honoré. *David and Goliath*, from *The Prayer Book of Philip IV the Fair*. 1296. (page 415)

How did the production of illuminated manuscripts change during the late thirteenth century? What did this new way of producing manuscripts lead to in the present day? How did this change lead to our ability to identify individual masters? How did Master Honoré of Paris alter the way figures were executed?

12.41. Jean Pucelle. *The Betrayal of Christ* and *Annunciation*, from the *Hours of Jeanne d'Évreux*. 1325–1328. (page 416)

Define:
  bas-de-page
  book of hours
  drôlleries
  grisaille

What did Jean Pucelle contribute to the art of illumination?

12.42. *Virgin of Jeanne d'Évreux*. 1339. (page 417)

How did the use of sculpture, especially in religious settings, change during the Late Gothic period?

Does the *Virgin of Jeanne d'Évreux* remind of works from the Middle Ages?

12.43. *Virgin of Paris.* Early 14th century. (page 418)

How is this work an extremely good example of Late Gothic figurative sculpture?

12.44. *Siege of the Castle of Love.* Back of a mirror. ca. 1320–1350. (page 418)

What makes this work an allegory?

12.45. Pierre Robin and Ambroise Harel. West façade, Saint-Maclou, Rouen, France. 1434–1490. (page 419)

Define:
  Flamboyant Phase

What declares that Saint-Maclou at Rouen is a flamboyant style church?

How does Flamboyant architecture relate to Late Gothic sculpture and painting?

12.46. Plan of Salisbury Cathedral, England. 1220–1265. (page 421)

Define:
   turret

Why aren't there very many fully Early English style churches?

What does the plan of Salisbury Cathedral retain?

12.47. Salisbury Cathedral (from the southwest) (spire ca. 1320–1330) (page 421)

What one cathedral is an exception to the fact that there aren't very many fully Early English style churches?

12.48. Nave, Salisbury Cathedral. (page 421)

How does the English Early Gothic style relate to the French form of Early Gothic?

12.49. Choir, Gloucester Cathedral, England. 1332–1357. (page 422)

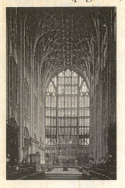

Define:
   Perpendicular Gothic style

How does the English Late Gothic style design ceilings? How do English Late Gothic style ceilings relate to the rest of the structure?

12.50. Chapel of Henry VII, Westminster Abbey, London, England. 1503–1519. (page 422)

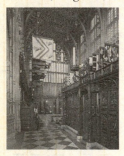

How does the Perpendicular Gothic style reach its apogee in Henry VII's chapel at Westminster Abbey?

12.51. *Jesus Teaching in the Temple* and *Hunting Scene*, from the *Queen Mary Psalter*. ca. 1310–1320. (page 423)

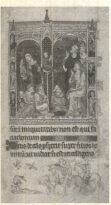

In what ways do these scenes from the *Queen Mary Psalter* retain elements of older English models while suggesting a general reliance on the French style?

12.52 Heinrich Parler the Elder and Peter Parler (?). Nave and Choir, Heiligenkreuz, Schwäbish-Gmünd, Germany. Begun 1317. (page 424)

Define:
  Hallenkirche

How does this church stem from Romanesque architecture while beginning to employ Gothic style?

12.53. Naumburg Master. *Crucifixion*, on the choir screen, and the *Virgin and John the Evangelist*. ca. 1255. (page 426)

Why was German Gothic sculpture less closely linked with architectural settings than French Gothic sculpture?

12.54. Naumburg Master. *The Kiss of Judas*, on the choir screen. ca. 1255. Naumburg Cathedral. (page 426)

What Classic period from antiquity can be thought of as a counterpart to the work of the Naumburg Master?

12.55. *Ekkehard and Uta*. ca. 1249–1255. Stone Naumburg Cathedral. (page 427)

Why were sculptures of *Ekkehard and Uta* installed at Naumburg Cathedral?

12.56. *Roettgen Pietà*. Early 14th century. (page 427)

Define:
   andachtsbild
   Pietà

How does the *Roettgen Pietà* help illustrate the kind of emotional fervor and mysticism that swept over fourteenth-century Europe?

12.57. Plan, Cathedral of Santa María, León, Spain. Begun 1240s. (Drawing by Giroux after De los Rios). (page 428)

The architect of Santa María, León was probably from what country?

12.58. Exterior, Cathedral of Santa María, León. (page 428)

What other cathedral is very reminiscent of Santa María, León?

12.59. Interior, Cathedral of Santa María, León. (page 429)

What do the lancet windows of Santa María, León have in common with the lancet windows of Sainte-Chapelle?

12.60. Jamb statue of *Simeon*, south portal of west façade, Cathedral of Santa María, León. ca. 1280–1300. (Page 430)

What other jamb statuary is related to the jamb statue of Simeon from the Cathedral of Santa María, León.

CHAPTER 13
Art in Thirteenth- and Fourteenth-Century Italy

Janson, pp. 432–463

While Italians had some of the same needs, fears and concerns as citizens of other areas of Europe, Italy was much closer geographically and philosophically to the Romans and Greeks of the ancient past and the Early Christian and Byzantine world of the recent past.

Throughout most of the Middle Ages the Holy Roman Empire and the papacy held political sway. The emperors lived far to the north and the papacy moved to France during the fourteenth century so hereditary rulers and leading merchant families wielded most of the power in the various city-states sprinkled across the Italian peninsula.

This independence combined with the extensive international travel of businessmen, church figures, thinkers, writers, artists and their patrons led to a growing interest in the accomplishments of individuals. The extensive study of ancient ideas, art and architecture led to the creation of the philosophy of Humanism. The application of these ideas to Italian art and architecture would lead to the Renaissance of the fifteenth century.

NOTES

CHURCH ARCHITECTURE AND THE GROWTH OF MENDICANT ORDERS

13.1. Nave and choir, Abbey Church of Fossanova, Italy. Consecrated 1208. (page 435)

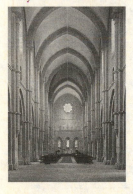

How does the Abbey Church of Fossanova exhibit the Cistercian plan?

13.2. Interior of Upper Church, Basilica of San Francesco, Assisi. Begun 1228; consecrated 1253. (page 435)

How does the interior (architecture, decoration and frescoes) of the Upper Church, Basilica of San Francesco, Assisi reflect the commitments of the Franciscan order?

13.3. Anonymous, *Saint Francis Preaching to the Birds*. 1290s (?). Basilica of San Francesco, Assisi. (page 436)

What is especially important about *Saint Francis Preaching to the Birds* and the other parts of the fresco cycle dedicated to the life story of Saint Francis? Is the designer and painter of this cycle known?

13.4. *Altarpiece of Saint Clare*. ca. 1280. Convent of Santa Chiara, Assisi. (page 436)

Why was this altarpiece dedicated to Saint Clare? What is the purpose of this altarpiece?

13.5. Nave and choir, Santa Croce, Florence. Begun ca. 1295. (page 437)

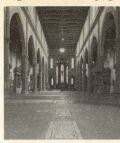

In what way does Santa Croce, Florence relate to Northern European Gothic standards?

13.6. Plan of Santa Croce. (page 437)

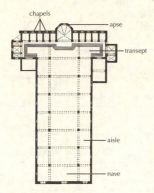

How does Santa Croce relate more to Italian standards such as those found in Italian Early Christian churches?

13.7. Nicola Pisano. Pulpit. 1259–1260. Baptistery, Pisa. (page 439)

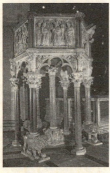

Describe the basic intent of the Pulpit of the Baptistry of Pisa.

13.8. *Fortitude*, detail of the pulpit by Nicola Pisano. 1260. (page 440)

What were Nicola Pisano's sources for the figure of Hercules? Why would a figure of Hercules be included with so many obviously Christian symbols?

13.9. *Nativity*, detail of the pulpit by Nicola Pisano. (page 440)

What inspired the images of the combined Annunciation and Nativity?

13.10. Giovanni Pisano. *The Nativity*, detail of pulpit. 1302–1310. Pisa Cathedral. (page 440)

How does Nicola's son interpret the nativity in this relief from the pulpit for the Cathedral of Pisa?

13.11. Florence Cathedral and Baptistery seen from the air. Cathedral begun 1296. (page 441)

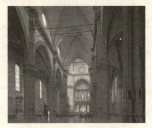

Define/Identify:
  campanile
  Duomo

Who were the architects for the Gothic cathedral and campanile?

13.12. Nave and choir, Florence Cathedral. (page 442)

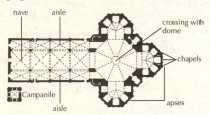

Identify the Northern Gothic elements incorporated into the Cathedral of Florence?

13.13. Plan of Florence Cathedral and Campanile. (page 442)

What particularly Italian features does the Cathedral of Florence contain?

13.14 Andrea da Pisano. South doors, Baptistery of San Giovanni, Florence. 1330–1336. (page 443)

What is the main subject of the panels in these bronze doors?

13.15. Andrea da Pisano. *The Baptism of Christ*, from the south doors, Baptistery of San Giovanni, Florence. 1330–1336. (page 444)

What is Gothic about these doors?

13.16. Palazzo della Signoria (Palazzo Vecchio), Florence. Begun 1298. (page 444)

Who probably designed the Palazzo della Signoria? What were the two main reasons for creating this structure?

13.17. Cimabue. *Madonna Enthroned*. ca. 1280–1290. (page 445)

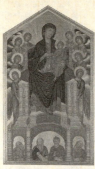

What seems to have been the greatest influence on the development of thirteenth and fourteenth century Italian painting?

Did some sort of synthesis take place?

Compare the *Madonna Enthroned* by Cimabue with the *Byzantine Madonna Enthroned* (8.50.) and the *Altarpiece of Saint Clare* (13.4.). What does Cimabue take from each source?

13.18. Giotto. *Madonna Enthroned*. ca. 1310. (page 445)

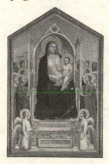

What does Giotto do in his *Madonna Enthroned* that begins to move Italian painting beyond Byzantine art? Is it evident that Giotto studied ancient models?

13.19. Interior, Arena (Scrovegni) Chapel. 1305–1306. Padua, Italy. (page 446)

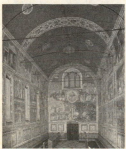

What are the major innovations of Giotto? How much of the interior of the Arena Chapel depends upon Giotto's fresco cycles?

Define:
  buon fresco
  fresco secco
  sinopia

Describe the basic buon fresco technique. Why would fresco secco be used with buon fresco?

13.20. Giotto. *Christ Entering Jerusalem*. 1305–1306. Arena (Scrovegni) Chapel. Padua, Italy. (page 446)

What did Giotto do in his *Christ Entering Jerusalem* to include the viewer?

Define:
  arriccio
  giornata

13.21. Giotto. *The Lamentation*. 1305–1306. Arena (Scrovegni) Chapel. Padua, Italy. (page 447)

What does Giotto perfectly match in his *Lamentation*?

13.22. Siena Cathedral, completed ca. 1260. Facade. Lower sections ca. 1284–1299 by Giovanni Pisano. (page 448)

What was the relationship between Florence and Siena?

Compare the Siena Cathedral to French Gothic models.

13.23. Duccio, *Virgin and Child*. ca. 1300. (page 449)

What models did Duccio probably look to while creating his *Virgin and Child*?

13.24. Duccio. *Madonna Enthroned*, center of the *Maestà Altar*. 1308–1311. (page 450)

What are the major influences evident in the *Madonna Enthroned* and the supporting panels?

13.25. Duccio. *Annunciation of the Death of the Virgin*, from the *Maestà Altar*. (page 451)

What synthesis takes place in Duccio's work?

13.26. Duccio. *Christ Entering Jerusalem*, from the back of the *Maestà Altar*. 1308–1311. (page 452)

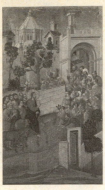

How is Duccio's Christ Entering Jerusalem different from Giotto's Christ Entering Jerusalem?

13.27. Simone Martini. *Annunciation*. ca. 1330. (page 453)

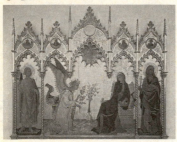

What did Simone Martini take from Giotto and what did he take from Duccio?

Where did Simone Martini spend the last part of his life?

13.28. Pietro Lorenzetti. *Birth of the Virgin*. 1342. (page 454)

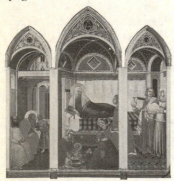

What did Pietro Lorenzetti do with the architecture of the painting and the frame? What did he learn from Duccio and what did he learn from Giotto?

13.29. Ambrogio Lorenzetti. *The Allegory of Good Government* (left). *Good Government in the City*, and portion of *Good Government in the Country* (right). 1338–1340. (page 455)

Did Ambrogio Lorenzetti utilize the same models that his brother Pietro did?

13.30. Ambrogio Lorenzetti. *Good Government in the City*. (page 455)

How did he use human beings in his *Good Government in the City* portion of his *Allegory of Good Government*?

13.31. Ambrogio Lorenzetti. *Good Government in the Country*. (page 457)

What does this painting utilize for the first time since Roman times? How is this scene different from its Roman models? What probably happened to Pietro and Ambrogio Lorenzetti?

13.32. Anonymous (Francesco Traini?). *The Triumph of Death* (detail). ca. 1325–1350. (page 457)

What occurred in the mid 1300s all across Europe to inspire works such as *The Triumph of Death* (detail)?

13.33. Andrea da Firenze, *Way of Salvation*. 1365–1367. (page 458)

What do the frescoes in the Guidalotti Chapel, Santa Maria Novella, Florence depict?

NORTHERN ITALY

13.34. Doge's Palace. Begun 1340. Venice. (page 459)

How is the Doge's palace in Venice different from the Palazzo della Signoria in Florence (13.16.)?

13.35. Milan Cathedral. Begun 1386. (page 460)

How does the form of Milan Cathedral relate to French Gothic architectural forms? What uniquely Italian features does it have?

13.36. Tomb of Bernabò Visconti. Before 1363. (page 461)

How does this tomb help explain the nature of Visconti rule in Milan? Does the equestrian nature of the portrait have antecedents in antiquity?

13.37. Giovannino dei Grassi, *Hours of Giangaleazzo Visconti*. ca. 1395. (page 462)

What style can be seen developing in this book of hours?

Why did Giangaleazzo Visconti commission this book of hours?